Surprising Bedfellows

Surprising Bedfellows

Hindus and Muslims in Medieval and Early Modern India

Edited by Sushil Mittal

LEXINGTON BOOKS
Lanham • Boulder • New York • Oxford

LEXINGTON BOOKS

Published in the United States of America
by Lexington Books
An imprint of The Rowman & Littlefield Publishing Group, Inc.
4501 Forbes Boulevard, Suite 200, Lanham, Maryland 20706

PO Box 317
Oxford
OX2 9RU, UK

British Library Cataloguing in Publication Information Available

Library of Congress Cataloging-in-Publication Data

Surprising bedfellows : Hindus and Muslims in medieval and early modern India / edited by Sushil Mittal.
p. cm.
ISBN: 978-0-7391-0673-0
1. India—Ethnic relations. 2. Hindus. 3. Muslims—India. 4. Hinduism—Relations—Islam. 5. Islam—Relations—Hinduism. 6. India—Civilization—18th century. I. Mittal, Sushil.

DS430.S88 2003
305.6'0954'0903—dc21 2003006909

Printed in the United States of America

™ The paper used in this publication meets the minimum requirements of American National Standard for Information Sciences—Permanence of Paper for Printed Library Materials, ANSI/NISO Z39.48–1992.

For Gene

Contents

Preface

Sushil Mittal

This volume is a collaborative effort in the best sense of the term. My first and greatest debt is to the very fine scholars whose writings are included in this book; all of them deeply committed to the exploration of Hindu-Islamic cultural interaction in India. I am also grateful to them for their invaluable suggestions and advice as the volume unfolded.

The chapters by Stewart Gordon, James W. Laine, Tony K. Stewart, and Phillip B. Wagoner were initially published in a special issue on 'Hindu as the Other of South Asian Islam' of the *International Journal of Hindu Studies* in 2000. As their contributions arrived in first draft, they were vetted by up to three specialist readers in each case; and, since all these specialists gave their time generously, I owe them a great debt of gratitude. I must also thank the contributors themselves for their patience and goodwill during this time-consuming process of writing and rewriting.

Robert I. Levy, Professor Emeritus of Anthropology at the University of California, San Diego, originally gave me the idea for this project, and to whom I owe a special thanks for much kindness and encouragement over the years. I would also like to extend my gratitude to my former colleagues at the Department of Religion, University of Florida, for their support, especially to Sheldon Isenberg; to two administrators at Millikin University with which I am currently affiliated, Stephen Fiol and late Robert C. McIntire, for their collegiality, friendship, and support; to Michael Kemery, a former student of Millikin University, for his assistance with knotty footnotes and bibliographic references and general research; to Ritu Mittal, my wife, for her extensive and meticulous proofreading; to Erik J. Hanson at AltaMira Press for his initial interest in this project; and to Serena Leigh Krombach, Martin Hayward, and Brian Richards at Lexington, for their support and enthusiasm for this project.

A final thank-you note is dedicated to Gene R. Thursby, who has been consistently supportive in many different areas.

Introduction

Peter Gottschalk

In January 2002, as India and Pakistan teetered on the brink of possibly their fourth full-scale war, the political leaders of both countries attended a regional meeting. The press, observant of secretive diplomatic efforts, questioned Pakistan's ruler, General Pervez Musharraf, regarding a recently reported interaction between two opposing officials. Musharraf, turning to his Foreign Minister, inquired, 'Sattar sahib, you weren't exchanging poems, were you?' (Dugger 2002: 1).

As Musharraf sought to leaven his diplomatic efforts with this remark, his Indian counterpart, Prime Minister Atal Vajpayee, portrayed the conflict in a manner meant to fit Western expectations: a militant Islamic state supportive of terrorists in the guise of Kashmiri freedom fighters assaults a secular, democratic state. Simultaneously, many Pakistanis replied that it was supporters of Vajpayee's Hindu nationalist political party who acted as terrorists as they threatened Muslims and Christians in India. The levity of Musharraf's comment might seem absurd before the growing specter of imminent warfare between such heavily armed neighbors who repeatedly referred to the possibility of a nuclear warfare endgame.

Yet, despite this rhetoric of otherness exchanged between powerful actors in an environment of rising mistrust and danger, Musharraf relied on a place of similitude upon which to pivot a joke. The practice of poetry exchange among some classes in North India and Pakistan allowed a space of participation uninterrupted, at least in his imagination, by the discordant rhythms of political strife. Indeed, a summit the previous year earlier included a *muśāyrā* (poetry gathering) for the mutual entertainment of Musharraf and Vajpayee (himself a poet) (Rafique 2001: 1).

The general's quip may have been afforded space in newspapers because it seemed so incongruous with the perceived realities of South Asian politics and cultures. Journalists and scholars have tended to view the subcontinent as partitioned primarily into divergent Hindu and Muslim communities that share nothing and contest most things. Their differences have molded, it is commonly reported, the politics and cultures of contestation and otherness for South Asia not only in its modern era but also since the Middle Period. The contributions to this volume describe Middle Period social worlds of Hindu-Muslim coexistence in which ethnic, class, and cultural concerns commonly eclipsed issues of religious difference. They recognize the wide range of affiliations Hindus and Muslims exercised and the shifting spheres of interaction where, for any individual at any particular moment, their religious identities may have been central, peripheral, or irrelevant. Finally, the authors offer alternative methods of interpreting contemporary materials that contest assumptions that have long led many European and American scholars to a bifurcated vision of the subcontinent. The reflex to sort social observations first through categories of religion immediately reduces nonreligious identities and interactions to an aberration. Through their challenge, the contributors deepen our understanding of this period at a time when this past is, perhaps, most contested.

Cultural arenas of Hindu-Muslim coexistence appear anomalous in South Asia only because our expectations are so often for difference and divergence. These expectations have developed within a worldview dominated, in the American academy, by post-Enlightenment thought. Since the eighteenth century, intellectual developments in Europe and the United States view humanity through a lens increasingly oriented toward the teleological vision that individualism, empiricism, nationalism, and secularism (among other ideologies) represent the most advanced articulations of social development. Borne on the success of the new technicalism, European merchants, discoverers, and officers increased the network of Western stations and factories in the Americas, Africa, Asia, Australia, and Oceania, thus allowing the expansion of Western economic involvement, political dominance, and cultural influence. In their global encounters, they inevitably compared other cultures with their own, and, from their perspective atop the mounting wave of European power, these Westerners more often than not found those subordinated, if not submerged, cultures wanting. This subjugation itself was explained commonly as the result of an inferior variation from Western cultural norms inherent in the indigenous society. If the non-Western individual failed to have the freedoms, recognition, and/or rights triumphed in Europe, then tribalism or despotism was believed to have crippled the society. If strife erupted that maimed the ability of members of a nation (an entity defined more often by the Western observers than indigenous participants), then these nationals had failed to learn how to sacrifice their sectarian differences on the altar of national interest. Chief among these divisive issues of the premodern mind was, of course, religion. The pervasiveness and durability of this overall view was amply demonstrated in domestic press coverage of the recent American war on Afghanistan that depicted Afghans, cultural cousins of South Asians, as citizens of a nation perpetually rent by tribal warfare fueled by a rampant religiosity that trampled human rights (defined in terms of the individual, not the community) and required Western interdiction and guidance.

Europeans, still sensitive to the memories of the turmoil and violence that raged across Europe following the Protestant Reformation (see Gordon), often believed their nations flourished, in part, because they had learned to safely contain—if not remove, as the secular ideal would have it in the United States—religion in the public realm. Westerners often concluded that other nations had yet to learn this lesson, relying unconsciously on an anticipation of progress that derived from Christian teleology. When the British first arrived on the subcontinent, they brought long memories of Christian European rivalry with Mediterranean Muslims and a romantic fascination with the idea of India. Their heavy reliance on the category of religion often led to a strict classification of South Asians primarily as 'Muhammadans' and 'Hindoos,' with an expectation that each category represented a discrete and complete realm of religion, society, and civilization. According to Western historiography that quickly set about discovering the history of India, the militant and decadent Muslim conquerors from beyond the Hindu Kush long ago had crushed the languid and sensual Hindu civilization. As the colonial British understood them, 'Indians' constituted a single nation suffering from inherent flaws that, under proper tutelage, they might learn to overcome.[1]

In their efforts to gain better economic, political, and military advantage of the land and 'its people,' the British employed all the resources of their epistemological tool case in order to 'know India.' The categories of knowledge and the classification schema used to sort and interpret data molded not only the reality the British perceived but also the social and political visions South Asians developed (see Bayly 1996; Cohn 1996; Inden 1990). The atlas for volume 26 of the *Imperial Gazetteer of India* (1931) demonstrates the interrelatedness of these fields of knowledge and the future ramifications of their acceptance by South Asians.

Projected upon a geographic outline of India and using multicolor shadings to depict the different classifications, the atlas illustrates natural (for example, geology and rainfall), economic (agriculture and railways), historical, and population features. Individual maps of the latter portray the composition of India according to race, language, and religion. These maps distilled the information garnered by linguistic, ethnographic, and archaeological surveys combined with the census of India. Arjun Appadurai (1996) has described the empirical and imperial project of the decadal censuses and their role in creating political realities for the emergent representational government in late colonial

India. In a foreshadowing of the future partition of India, the green areas on the religion map depicting Muslim-dominated regions almost perfectly matches the present borders of Pakistan, the fraternal twin conceived seemingly as evidence of the dangers of public religion and reluctantly delivered by the British. Not only did the epistemological practices and social ideologies employed by the British prove their expectations (e.g., Muslim and Hindu cultures are irreconcilable), but, once appropriated by residents, they molded South Asian self-perceptions as well. Thus, many Hindu nationalists currently uphold themselves as true secularists as they campaign against the pseudo-secularism of programs intended to ensure representational involvement of religious minorities in government. Meanwhile, their reverence for Hinduism references a term unknown before the early nineteenth century: yet another product of British epistemological categorization and South Asian appropriation (King 1999: 100). The historical maps, derived from the discipline of historiography that South Asians would also appropriate with little metacritical perspective, demonstrates again how the British saw Indians and themselves so differently in terms of religion with each territory of the myriad opposing states shaded either yellow for Hindu, green for Muhammadan, or red for British (note, not Christian).

In Europe and the United States, descriptions of South Asia have remained reliant on the attribution of religious identity to individuals, cultures, and states with little critical reflection on how religion figures into Western epistemologies. As Eric Sharpe (1986: 121) has detailed, Europeans did not create a lens for the study of religion distinct from their theological reading glasses until the Dutch Universities Act replaced Christian dogmatics and practical theology with the history of religions at four state universities in 1877. Developed in concert with the increasing secularization of many societies, the secular study of religion often understands religion as a detachable element of society. In the United States, secular concerns often forbid the inclusion of religious studies in public school curricula, thus ensuring for generations of students that religion seems as though it naturally and most safely exists only in the private realm of home and house of worship. Religions that resist this partitioning and find their way into the public life of economics and politics no longer seem to be religions but something more. As so many primers and documentaries intone, 'Islam [or Hinduism] is not just a religion but a way of life.'

As life ways informed by religious identities, 'Hindu' and 'Muslim' cultures appear more intractable and nonintegrated than ever, seeming to be entire and complete spheres of social identity and interaction. And, so, South Asia appears to be a subcontinent of multiple yet nonoverlapping cultural realms that, with the inevitability of plate tectonics, must grind against one another's absolute and impenetrable borders. The juxtapositions are familiar: Muslims eat the cows revered by Hindus; Hindus venerate icons reviled by Islamic doctrine; Muslim men circumcise their penises, while Hindu men pierce their ears.

Academics have structured educational programs according to these expectations, and their institutions, in turn, perpetuate them. It is common that graduate students in fields associated with South Asia have to choose quickly their cultural and, by implication, religious area: Arabic and Urdu or Bengali for studies of Muslim cultures and Sanskrit and Hindi, Bengali, or a South Indian language for studies of Hindu cultures. If their advisors do not ensure conformity, then the job market often does. Most religious studies departments, until recently, have almost uniformly advertised specifically for specialists in a particular religion and sought curriculum established around traditions understood to be self-contained and entirely discrete.

Nevertheless, more recent scholarship has sought to challenge many of these long-standing and increasingly perilous perspectives. Nita Kumar (1989) recognized the multiple identities of the Ansārī weavers of present-day Banaras, analyzing them as artisans, Muslims, and Banarsis. She demonstrated that, far from being an entirely discreet, self-contained group, Ansārīs share identities with members of other groups in various contexts. Following the tragic destruction of the so-called Babri Masjid in Ayodhya by Hindu militants in 1992, the consequent communal riots, and the subsequent electoral success of Hindu nationalism, many more scholars have interrogated the role of scholarship in fueling the communal imagination. To mention but a few of these efforts, Richard Eaton (1993), critiquing the notion that the expansion of South Asia's Muslim population resulted primarily from forced conversion, carefully outlines the gradual process by which many members of the indigenous population through contact with Ṣūfīs may have come to associate and then replace their deities with Islamic monotheism. Using epigraphic evidence, Cynthia Talbot (1995) challenges previous depictions of intractably sparring religious kingdoms in Middle Period Andhra. She demonstrates that Hindu inscriptions represented Muslims in myriad ways and those meant to condemn Muslim political opponents relied primarily on ethnic, not religious, charicatures of difference. My own work (Gottschalk 2000) has sought to explore the multiple identities with which individuals belong to a variety of groups—devotional and otherwise—as evidenced in narratives from contemporary rural Bihar. The social memories of village residents reflect self-identities and social interactions too fluid and complex for the categories of Hindu and Muslim to encapsulate.

Despite these recent forays into this enduring problem, many dilemmas of cultural interpretation for Western scholars remain deeply embedded. The contributors to this volume superbly demonstrate a number of alternatives that not only challenge prevailing paradigms but also offer the models necessary to shift them. They employ in-depth research with far-reaching implications using historiographic, literary, and art historical methods to understand Middle Period South Asia. Collectively, this refinement of interpretation pivots on the following interrelated themes: terminology, convergence, fluidity, and contextuality.

Perhaps the most challenging of the issues that the authors undertake deals with terminology. They each ask what implications and alternatives there are for descriptors such as 'Hindu,' 'Muslim,' 'Indic,' and 'Islamic,' and the categorization system that the terms imply. In particular, each author has chosen to focus on a cultural convergence which demonstrates the inadequacy of these terms while highlighting one of the shortcomings of the dominant Western hermeneutic of cultural interpretation.

Phillip Wagoner's description of a building constructed using Indic style and serving Muslim ritual needs demonstrates both a convergence of cultural patterns and insufficiency (if not danger) of any single descriptor. His caution is worth quoting: 'If we arbitrarily decide to call it either a mosque or a *dharmasāle* alone, then we have fallen unwittingly into the intellectual straightjacket of communalism and failed to achieve our goal of a historical understanding of the past' (p.49). Wagoner here uncovers a seldom perceived pitfall among attempts to counter communalist rhetoric. That is, in their effort to wrestle against communalist conclusions, scholars often rely on the overly simplistic descriptors and characterizations employed by communalists and so reinforce their use. As an example, the phrase 'Hindu-Muslim coexistence' I use above to counter arguments of complete separatism suggests the unity and discreteness of two social realms, erasing overlap while attempting to demonstrate interaction.

The other authors also relate instances of convergence to demonstrate the inadequacy of interpretations that rely solely on such descriptors. In his explorations of the romances involving Satya Pīr, Tony Stewart describes how sometimes narratives equate Allāh with Nārāyaṇa-Viṣṇu, while, in other moments, the Pīr explains to a devotee that no difference exists between the Vedas, the Purāṇas, and the Qur'ān. Stewart attributes the failure of scholarship to properly comprehend texts that fall between Hindu and Muslim cultural spheres to an overreliance on sociological interpretative methods that concern themselves too deeply with communalist ideologies. He argues that literary analysis privileges the inventiveness of the text beyond the narrowness of ideological categories.

In a similar vein, James Laine argues that both communalists and secularists fail to adequately grasp the complexity of the situation. While the first see different religions as dominating separate social realms, the second consider religion in this period to be secondary to an inclusive universalism. The hagiographies of Śivājī that he examines demonstrate a far more complex and fluid situation in which a Hindu author can depict a Muslim as both 'other' and 'natural' in the very same text. These examples demonstrate the possibilities of simultaneous convergence and divergence of interest and identity between an author and any individual she or he might describe.

Stewart Gordon's theoretical approach to otherness explores this issue on the level of Middle Period state politics. He challenges the appropriateness of not only labeling states in northern Maharashtra and central India as 'Hindu' and 'Muslim' but also of suggesting the category of 'other' at all. Both derive from Western expectations of religious exclusion and conflict, originating in the experiences of Reformation Europe and obscuring the convergence of interests and consequential relations between state, religion, and institutions in South Asia. The Mughals and Marāṭhās both supported Hindu and Muslim holy figures and religious institutions. When patronage diminished this had more to do with altering political situations than increasing religious chauvinism. Although these states may have attributed to themselves a religious identification, they did so less from ideological commitment than political expediency. Integral to this argument is Gordon's awareness of fluidity. The author's focus on the changes within political formations and policies allows him to recognize that, rhetoric notwithstanding, states relied too heavily on an inherently integrated society as well as Hindu and Muslim institutions to jeopardize their rule through ideologically chauvinistic exclusions or expulsions.

Wagoner echoes this theme as he explains that the religious rituals and rhetoric of Deccan states often must be interpreted not as ideological commitments to exclusivity but as the language (oral and physical) of official transactions. With the examples of biographies of one official and a mosque patronized by another, he demonstrates the fluidity within certain social circles that extended between states. This not only allowed individuals of a certain class endowed with specific skills to move between employment opportunities in Hindu and Muslim states irrespective of their personal religion, it fostered in them the ability to engage in the diverse symbolic and practical interactions required in this multicultural world. This fluidity not only allowed for individuals of such abilities to find opportunities in various cultural environments but also required them to be professionally involved with members of other classes and cultures in a variety of kingdoms. The patron who financed the construction of a mosque, therefore, also interacted with the artisans and engravers involved in its construction.

Stewart, meanwhile, emphasizes fluidity in the realm of fiction. In his emphasis on literary interpretations of the texts, he argues that the literary imagination is far less constrained than doctrine and theology. This allows portrayals of the negotiations through which the characters navigate a social world not simply bifurcated into Hindu and Muslim spheres. Hence, the romances demonstrate a complicated Bengali social realm involving far more opportunities and interactions than admitted by purely ideological descriptions or analyses.

Similarly focused on literature, Laine engages the notion of fluidity on the level of identity, recognizing that religious identity and terms had different meanings relative to social context. Examining the Marathi hagiographic literature of Śivājī, he observes 'otherness' resulted only as part of certain rhetorical strategies, not sociopolitical realities. In fact, the fluidities of folk cultures and religions disallowed the absolute boundaries necessary for such artificial definitions of otherness in everyday life. However, following the course of hagiographic development, he tracks the changes in the depiction of the Marāṭhā leader in his struggle against Muslim armies first as that of Arjuna fighting family and close friends and then as Rāmā challenging the demonic host of the *Rāmāyaṇa*.

Overall, each of the authors argues for a refashioning of the hermeneutic used in their respective fields that better contextualizes the objects of research. This requires the recognition that Middle Period South Asia represents a more complicated sphere of interaction, convergence, and fluidity than present terminology and scholarship often acknowledges. These authors most provocatively challenge contemporary scholars as they demonstrate what recent interpretations have *failed* to see. Research has overlooked the administrative support for religious institutions that did not conform to the state religion in Middle Period Maharashtra. Scholars did not recognize Aḥmad Khān's *dharmsāle* (a building of Indic design with a Sanskrit label) in Vijayanagara as a mosque until the 1980s. The Bengali romances of Satya Pīr escaped attention because they defied categorization as 'Hindu' or 'Muslim.' The rhetoric of 'other' in seventeenth- and eighteenth-century Maharashtra duped researchers to ignore the commonplace acceptance of Hindu kingship under Muslim rule. Perhaps only more amazing than the complexity of the social negotiations that gave rise to these examples is the utter naturalness with which many South Asians apparently navigated, on multiple levels, interreligious and intercultural transactions. This was (and, in many similarly overlooked ways, still is) quite simply, their cultural context.

The contributors to this volume demonstrate that the primacy of religion and the classifications of 'Hindu' and 'Muslim,' 'Indic,' and 'Islamic' are increasingly problematic as assumptions for the diligent interpreter of Middle Period South Asia. This period, dominated in the Western imagination by the likes of Awrangzīb and Śivājī—those prototypical communalists—is better characterized by a fluidity of social movement and inclusion in many spheres. We need to deepen our understanding of the cultural situation and the contextual use of contemporary terminology with full awareness of the distortive effects of our own cultural worldviews and applied epistemologies. No one observes without a lens of inherent limitations—we are blamelessly of our own cultures.

But as cultural interpreters our difficult burden requires us to understand the complexities on both sides of the lens we choose.

Notes

1. The continuity of this view of Indian singularity can be seen in the durability in English, at least, of the label 'India' for the entire subcontinent and the adjective 'Indian' for South Asia's natural and cultural components.

References Cited

Appadurai, Arjun. 1996. "Number in the Colonial Imagination." In, *Modernity at Large: Cultural Dimensions of Globalization,* 114–35. Minneapolis: University of Minnesota Press.

Bayly, C. A. 1996. *Empire and Information: Intelligence Gathering and Social Communication in India, 1780–1870.* Cambridge: Cambridge University Press.

Cohn, Bernard. 1996. *Colonialism and Its Forms of Knowledge: The British in India.* Princeton: Princeton University Press.

Dugger, Celia. 2002. "Leaders of India and Pakistan Share a Stage, Not a Solution." *The New York Times* (January 8) <http://www.nytimes.com/2002/01/07/international/asia/07INDI.html?pagewanted=print>.

Eaton, Richard. 1993. *The Rise of Islam and the Bengal Frontier, 1204–1760.* Delhi: Oxford University Press.

Gottschalk, Peter. 2000. *Beyond Hindu and Muslim: Multiple Identity in Narratives from Village India.* New York: Oxford University Press.

Inden, Ronald. 1990. *Imagining India.* Cambridge: Blackwell.

King, Richard. 1999. *Orientalism and Religion: Post-colonial Theory, India, and 'the Mystic East.'* New York: Routledge.

The Imperial Gazetteer of India. 1931. *The Imperial Gazetteer of India.* Volume 26: *Atlas.* Oxford: Clarendon.

Kumar, Nita. 1989. "Work and Leisure in the Formation of Identity: Muslim Weavers in a Hindu City." In, *Culture and Power in Banaras: Community, Performance, and Environment, 1800–1980*, 147–70. Berkeley: University of California Press.

Rafique, Mohammad. 2001. "The Poets, Too, Had Their Day." *Dawn* (July 19) <http://www.dawn.com/2001/07/19/fea.htm>.

Sharpe, Eric. 1986. *Comparative Religion: A History.* La Salle: Open Court.

Talbot, Cynthia. 1995. "Inscribing the Other, Inscribing the Self: Hindu-

Muslim Identities in Pre-colonial India." *Society for Comparative Study in Society and History* 37, 4: 692–722.

Hindus, Muslims, and the Other in Eighteenth-Century India

Stewart Gordon

LOCATING ALTERITY

Let us begin the discussion by suggesting some historical background of the term 'other.' Specifically, I would like to suggest four historicized locations of the word, each of which has its focus and uses.

The first location of 'other' was whoever existed beyond the geographic edge of the known world. This usage has a long history and probably a prehistory. Bards, travelers, and authors described this other-beyond-the-known-world in semifactual, semifabulous terms with a set of characteristics—cultural, societal, emotional, physical—which defined the other as alien, foreign, 'not us,' therefore, both fascinating and terrible. In Western literature, Herodotus exemplifies this tradition, especially in his writing of the Persians as 'not-Greeks' (see Hartog 1988).[1] The Odyssey illustrates that one's reaction to the other need not be fear and hostility; Ulysses survived by the kindness of strangers, and the story can be read as a common humanity beneath the strangeness of the other. This lively tradition of other-beyond-the-known-world continued, for example, in Pliny's semifabulous geography and Cicero's discussion of *civis* and those beyond who did not participate in *civis*; it continued through Abū 'Abd Allāh Muḥammad Ibn Bāṭūṭah's and Marco Polo's narratives, Spanish descriptions of the New World, the voyages of Lemuel Gulliver, and early colonial writing on Africa and Asia. It is alive and well in the writings of Joseph Conrad, Edward Forster, and Rudyard Kipling. In Forster's *Passage to India* (1924), for example, the sympathetic British know quite a lot about the Indians they rule—what they eat, how they dress, who they marry, what they hope for. Nevertheless, this knowledge sits above essential, unhistorical, unchangeable, and unknowable differences that make empathy impossible and the other seem monstrous or inhuman.

The other-beyond-the-known-world has, of course, been the realm of anthropology (and 'race science') for the last century. In recent decades, many have questioned the very foundations of anthropology with its focus on a non-European, exotic otherness (see Bhabha 1990; Fabian 1983; Geertz 1988; Inden 1990; Said 1978). Much of the recent writing on colonial India, following Frantz Fanon (1963) and Antonio Gramsci (1991), envisions hegemony and resistance as the only possible relation between the colonizing other and indigenous peoples.

The second use of the term 'other' locates it within a culture and refers to the relations between the dominant group and various marginalized groups. Even though they move amongst us, as other they are alien, foreign, and 'not us.' Jews and Gypsies, women and nomads, were all treated as others in European literature. Shylock asks, 'If you cut us, do we not bleed?' in an attempt to break down the divide that separated him from his non-Jewish accusers. As in the first location of other, this other-among-us has a large literature and a long history. Let me suggest some themes in this tradition. The nineteenth century spawned studies of vagrants, madmen, and ethnic minorities. In England, we find well-known studies of prostitutes, criminals, and the working poor. This other-among-us tradition has yielded an extraordinary variety of studies and theoretical approaches. For example, American sociology moved in the direction of numeric data, conditions, social markers, behaviors, group characteristics, and perceptions (see Harrington 1962). Sociology and social psychology now have questionnaires which routinely test characteristics of self and social distance from other.

Equally useful, though very different, are histories of how the dominant culture marginalized other-among-us by exorcism and exclusion. For example, in Michel Foucault's *Madness and Civilization* (1965), the dominant European culture defined its characteristics as reason; the other (madness = unreason) had no characteristics and was therefore worthless. Unreason deserved confinement and annihilation. Foucault's use of the other alerts us that the construction is fraught with ideological and power implications.

The third location of other is whatever exists at the opposite end of a one-on-one relationship between one human consciousness and another. Again, I make no attempt at an etymology, only a few suggestions of development of this location. Immanuel Kant (1933) stated the problem: How do we know anything about a sentient being we might observe? Georg Hegel suggested that there was no problem because there was no independent other, only a reflection and expansion of the 'I' (see Dostal 1997; Harris 1997; Klemm and Zoler 1969; Marcuse 1954). More recent philosophers (Buber 1937; Heidegger 1949; Sartre 1964) have discussed what is meant by this 'annihilation' of the other and posed various alternatives to Hegel's formulation with various shades of optimism or (mostly) pessimism concerning whether it is possible to connect with another consciousness. Throughout, this location of the 'problem' of the other is interpersonal, centered on the reducibility or nonreducibility of other to self, focused on the individual rather than a group and located within a culture rather than at its margins (see Corbey and Leersen 1991).

The fourth location of the other is within a person. This usage has too long and complex an etymology for more than a cursory treatment. In many cultures, there is the tradition of spirit possession by the other, who holds information and advice not known by his vessel. The other-within went by many names in European tradition—evil, satanic possession, dark forces, witchcraft. In more recent terminology, Sigmund Freud's id is the other-within. It defines what seems alien, foreign, and 'not me' about myself, the wild, primitive, internalized other, both familiar and dangerous. It is the 'Steppenwolf' of Hermann Hesse. The uses of this fourth location, other-within, are quite different from the first three. It focuses on mental health and therapy. Quantification, history, and social policy are not part of its primary function.

The vastly proliferated literature on 'identity' of the last twenty years has produced complex and often contradictory formulations in its use of other. Let me suggest some of the problems with the term. Is other a set of characteristics —social, emotional, physical—that 'they' have and 'we' do not (an essentialist position)? Are all notions of identity and other fluid, contested, fragmented, and uncompleted (a constructivist position)? Does the other have an essentialized network of social relationships that 'we' do not (a relational approach)? Does dislike of the other constitute a large part of 'our' identity (an emotionalist position)? Does the state have a hegemonic role in the formation of identity (a paranoia position)? Is the other outside the institutional network that 'we' support (an institutionalist position)? Does everyone need an 'identity' and an other for mental health (a psychologist position)? Is 'identity' the basis for politics (a political scientist position)? Given the sharply different definitions and uses, I have chosen not to use the term 'identity' in this chapter. Rather, I will try to discuss relations between Hindus and Muslims from the locations of other in the discussion above.

On the face of it, location number one does not seem relevant for a discussion of Hindus and Muslims in eighteenth-century India. Far from either group being beyond-the-edge-of-the-known-world, both shared the same world. Locations three and four also seem irrelevant; the question seems not to be the mental health or personal alienation of members of one group. In fact, only the second, other-among-us, seems relevant to Muslims and Hindus in the eighteenth century. Within this location, theory developed by sociology and social psychology seems particularly attractive. Unlike Foucault, the hypotheses are often 'middle range,' that is, they do not require the positing of vast epochs, such as the Age of Reason or the Modern Age. Also, these disciplines have spent a great deal of effort to operationalize the concepts of social distance and its converse, the sense of community; they focus our attention on specific disprovable hypotheses tightly attached to theory. Further, this body of research allows us to look at behaviors, outcomes, and data more than textuality.

I find particularly useful the recent work of Per Otnes, a Norwegian philosopher of sociology. In *Other-wise* (1997), he suggests, following Sartre and Talcott Parsons, that the problems we have with self, other, and identity as concepts stem from trying to make them independent variables, when in fact the fundamental unit of analysis should be a triadic relationship. Specifically, Otnes proposes a unit of analysis that connects self and other by means of a 'mediator'—generally an artifact that both self and other, to some degree, 'share.' Otnes's definition of a mediating artifact is quite wide, including, for example, a tool, a relative, a contract, a book, or a restaurant. Analysis centers on an interconnected, multivalent network that includes selves, others, and mediators. This viewpoint takes us away from essentialist problems of self and other, allowing both to be different, depending on the mediator. It also suggests a means for the more interesting constructivist position which sees both self and other as works-in-progress. Finally, it connects both self and other to the socially constructed material world, a position lacking in identity discourse on textuality.

THE 'OTHER' WORLD OF LATE SIXTEENTH-CENTURY EUROPE

Following Otnes, we first turn to a brief analysis of self, other, and mediator in Europe from the Treaty of Augsburg to the Thirty Years' War. Interesting is the power of the categories 'Catholic' and 'Protestant' to eliminate or erase expected mediations between selves and others. Put more simply, Protestant and Catholic defined political, economic, cultural, and intellectual life. The Augsburg treaty physically divided Europe between Catholic and Protestant states; each prince had to choose one or the other. Promptly, Protestant princes seized Catholic properties in their kingdoms. The Peace of Augsburg hardly slowed the all-out conflict. Shortly after Augsburg, the Council of Trent defined 'belief' and 'heresy,' rejecting all compromise. Philip II reassured the Pope in 1568 that he would crush the Protestant rebellion in the Netherlands and 'neither danger to myself nor the ruin of these states, nor of all the others that are left to me, will prevent me from doing what a Christian God-fearing prince ought to do' (Maland 1980: 6; see also Munck 1990; Polisensky 1971). Thirty years and countless lives later, Philip was still trying.

Religious cleavage mattered in such a fundamental way that much of society's fears and angers, its everyday life and politics, revolved around two other categories. We should remember that Protestantism was a specific ideological repudiation of the spiritual authority of Rome and was, in the tradition of other heresies, most brutally suppressed. Both Catholic and Protestant represented all that the other hated, feared, and suspected. Dress bifurcated, with Protestants favoring severe dark colors and white; Catholics favored bright colors and as much finery as the purse permitted. Military alliances strictly followed religion; military recruitment largely did. Religious tracts railed against the other. The Catholic index of prohibited books denied Protestant texts to Catholic areas. Towns and town councils were either Catholic or Protestant. Trade patterns followed religious cleavages. Catholic Spain, for example, closed all of its empire to Protestant England and Holland. England and Holland, in return, raided Spanish shipping and forced the opening of Spanish ports. There were riots and killings of the other in both Catholic and Protestant areas; expulsions and attempts to seize areas and forcibly convert citizens (such as Cologne, 1582) were common. The numerous wars in Middle and Eastern Europe were mainly over enclaves of one religion or the other. Recall that there were four religious civil wars in France in this period and an attempted Catholic restoration in England which was ruthlessly suppressed.

Large states with both Catholic and Protestant populations were paralyzed; the Hapsburg Diet could no longer function. Protestant states no longer recognized Catholic-dominated Hapsburg courts. When the Austro-Hungarian emperor ordered the expulsion of all Protestant preachers from Vienna and restricted Protestant worship throughout the empire, peasant revolts broke out periodically: 'After about 1560, Catholics and Protestants had no interest in spiritual or intellectual reconciliation.... Each side sought to convert the other by sheer brute force' (Dunn 1970: 8).

If anything, by the first decades of the seventeenth century, attitudes hardened and armed leagues formed on religious lines. Although various treaties and other interests mitigated, they did not reverse this trend. (As a suggestion of how deep and pervasive this cleavage remained, let me remind the reader that the practice of Catholicism was illegal in Protestant Switzerland until 1848 and that Catholics were barred from public office, elected or civil, in England until 1829; Hughes 1975: 274.)

Here, indeed, we have a striking phenomenon, a set of religious categories so strong that they erased most of the normal mediators between selves who were Protestant and others who were Catholic. This historical period gives us a series of rough and ready indices by which we can measure social distance between groups, one which will prove useful in our examination of eighteenth-century India, to which we now turn.

SOCIAL DISTANCE IN EIGHTEENTH-CENTURY INDIA

Let us now look for some of these 'erasure of mediators' in eighteenth-century India. Kings were of course either Muslim or Hindu, but all of the remaining conditions simply were not present. There is no pattern of Hindu states allying with other Hindu states in preference to allying with Muslim states.[2]

Routine measures against the other in Europe were also absent. No Muslim or Hindu enclaves were seized; populations were not expelled on the basis of religion. No prince publicly committed himself and all of his resources to the annihilation of the other. Both Hindus and Muslims were routinely and without comment recruited into all armies of the period.

There is no evidence of trade following religion. To the contrary, every major banking house had branches in all the major cities—whether the ruler was Hindu or Muslim. Credit moved just as easily between Muslim Allahabad and Hindu Indore as it did between Muslim Allahabad and Muslim Hyderabad. While there were occasional tracts railing against Muslims (such as the *Śivabhārata*), these are matched by mirror-of-princes documents (the *Ajñapatra*) that did not even single out Muslims as a category of subjects to worry about. Unlike the Europe we have considered, nowhere in India in the eighteenth century did any king attempt to overthrow another reigning house for the purpose of installing a fellow religionist. Nor did they experience population expulsions, religious riots, or forced conversions. No king ever ordered that the Hindu or Muslim faith could not be preached or practiced in his borders.

Unlike Europe, states containing large numbers of both Hindus and Muslims were not paralyzed by strife. Quite to the contrary, courts functioned, precedent remained in place, and contracts were honored. Unlike Europe, both Hindus and Muslims continued to serve in the governments of kings of the other religion. In sum, after considering a true other situation based on religion in seventeenth-century Europe, what strikes one about eighteenth-century India is the social closeness rather than the social distance. Virtually none of the measures of religious cleavage found in seventeenth-century Europe were present in eighteenth-century India. It is only against this broad background of social closeness that the Marāṭhā documents that concern Muslims make sense.

THE DOCUMENTS

Let us now turn to the specifics of what happened when an area moved from control by a Muslim kingdom to control by a Hindu kingdom. For some years, I have been working on fine-grid revenue documents of the city of Burhanpur (on the Tāptī River on the northern border of Maharashtra) and the *ṣūba* of Khandesh (an administrative unit of several hundred villages that runs westward along the Tāptī River towards Gujarat). Burhanpur had a long history as a Muslim capital beginning with the Fārūqī dynasty in the early fifteenth century. By the early decades of the eighteenth century, it had been a Mughul capital, a Mughul regional center, and a regional base for the Niẓām of Hyderabad. In short, it was a city dominated by a great central mosque; the large Muslim population supported itself mainly by weaving fine cotton cloth with gold threads for which the city was famous.

Marāṭhā documents on Khandesh begin in 1721; by military success and subsequent treaty, Marāṭhās began 'dual administration' with the Niẓām. The Marāṭhās were entitled to *cauth* and *sardeśmukhī* (in effect, 35 percent of the government's share of the revenue) and sent their own collectors into the countryside to do settlement and collection.[3]

Initial Marāṭhā documentation was scrappy but became progressively better, more detailed and predictable, through the next three decades. By the time that the Marāṭhās actually won Burhanpur in the 1750s as a result of a military victory over the Niẓām, they knew what documentation they needed to rule. As part of the peace treaty, the Niẓām's administrators turned over a variety of tax and revenue documents, both normative and actual, which the Marāṭhās copied into Modi script and carefully preserved. Thus, we find accounts—often down to daily transactions—of the income from mint and market, fines and transit duties, and the minutiae of government expenditure from the mid-1750s until well into the nineteenth century. From these documents, we get a clear picture of what it meant for the area to move from the 'Muslim' administration of Mughuls and the Niẓām to the 'Hindu' administration of the Marāṭhās and their Brāhmaṇa administrators.

CONTINUITIES UNDER MARĀṬHĀ RULE

The glory days of Burhanpur were long over by the middle decades of the eighteenth century. Nevertheless, the city remained an important provincial capital and a trading and manufacturing center, especially for cloth. It was also an important transshipping point for goods moving between north and Surat.

What of the structure of trade, the lifeblood of the city, after Marāṭhā conquest? What is unexpected is that under Marāṭhā rule, Muslims retained certain trade advantages which they had under the Mughul administration. Specifically, a Musalman paid 2.5 percent *ad valorem* transit duty, while a Hindu paid 5 percent. This differential remained in place throughout the eighteenth century. Similar differentials remained in place for those Musalmans bringing bullion or old coins to the mint; the duties were twice as high for a Hindu. These tax advantages were however not universal. All dealers, regardless of religion, paid the same duties on, for instance, vegetables, timber, services, and shops (PK no. 118, Jhaḍtī of 1763–64). Thus, the overall pattern was distinct tax advantages for Muslims engaged in long-distance, high-value trade or bankers needing coinage. Local Muslim traders in hinterland-to-city staples had no particular advantage.

The group likely to benefit from such advantages was, in fact, Burhanpur's single most powerful group of traders under Mughul rule, the Bohora Muslims; they remained dominant right through Marāṭhā rule. There are two interesting points about these tax advantages: (1) We find evidence of these advantages for Muslims continuing at other sites in the Marāṭhā domains, such as Ahmedabad (SSRPD 3: 321). (2) These urban documents are the only administrative documents of the Marāṭhās I have ever seen that use the actual terms 'Musalmān' and 'Hindū'—nowhere else, not in judicial cases, not in other revenue documents, not in letters.

Besides trading patterns, government religious patronage also shows remarkable continuity from the Niẓām's 'Muslim' administration to the Marāṭhā 'Hindu' one. Detailed accounts of the city of Burhanpur during the first years of Marāṭhā administration in the 1760s give a remarkably clear picture of religious patronage during this period. Deep in the yearly summary of expenditure, we find a category entitled 'Monthly wages,' dominated by Muslim recipients. In the same document, the category of 'Miscellaneous *faqīrs*' included twenty-six men, all Muslims. The government also allotted money for the celebrations of Muḥarram and Ramaḍān (including the Qur'ān recitation), the expenses of turbans for the celebration of Īd, and the *qāẓī*'s fee on these occasions.

We should not, however, have the impression that the Marāṭhā government was only supporting Muslim religious men and festivals. Quite to the contrary, in this same document, listed right along with the Muslim recipients were seventy-nine Brāhmaṇas; as well as cash grants for the ceremonies of Brāhmaṇas to ward off an inauspicious day and for new moon ceremonies, Saṅkrānta, Dīvālī, Daśaharā, Śivarātri, and Gaṇeśa Caturthī and small contributions for temple expenses in Burhanpur (PK no. 196; see also SPD 4, selection

102).[4]

A few years later, in 1765, we receive a more complete list of grantees, in a section entitled 'Miscellaneous people as per the assignment register.' Of the 338 men given grants, most were Muslims and over 100 were *faqīrs*, *shaykhs*, or *qāẓīs*. Salaries varied, from more than 400 rupees per year down to only a few rupees per year (PK no. 119).

In the hinterland of Burhanpur, the most important indigenous officials were known as *deśmukhs* ('mouth of the land'). It was these powerful, local militarized families that stood responsible for the year's taxes and were the focal point for remissions in drought or disaster and resistance to unjust demands. Scattered among the mainly Hindu *deśmukhs* (of many different castes) were a few Muslim families. After the Marāṭhā takeover, these Muslim *deśmukhs* were not displaced; rather, they signed and honored the same contracts which the Hindu *deśmukhs* did.

Also in the hinterland of Burhanpur, a variety of 'worthy' men were supported through *aima* grants (maintenance grants for persons of learning or merit). Let us look specifically the Parganā of Adilabad (an administrative unit of slightly over one hundred villages located thirty miles west of Burhanpur along the Tāptī Valley). Consider a contract of *aima* from the village of Khadke, Adilabad Parganā, from 1739 which gives all the typical details of this type of grant:

> The marked ground of 100 *bīghās* of Ḥājī Ibrāhīm is fixed at 1 and 3/4 less [than the standard rate of taxation]. For uncultivated land, 1 *ṭakā* and 1 *rukh* [per *bīghā*]; for cultivated land, no *ṭakās* and 4 *rukhs* [per *bīghā*]. It is given to him to cultivate. Therefore the *ṭakās* are fixed at 39 (PK no. 194; my translation).[5]

Note a number of features of this sort of grant. First, it was a development grant; taxes were much lower on the cultivated land than the uncultivated. Second, the land was still taxed, though at a much lower than standard rate. Third, the rate was fixed, so that benefits of cultivation accrued much more to the grantee than the government.

A document from 1748 shows *aima* grants in 17 of Adilabad's 108 cultivated villages (PK no. 194). The register lists slightly more than a hundred recipients by name; the amount of land granted to them, whether it was cultivated or not; what offices, if any, the recipient held; and, incidentally, the signature of the local official involved.

Fascinating is the complete intermixture of Hindus and Muslims within this originally Muslim institution for support of 'worthy' or 'learned' men. Note also the year, 1748; this was well before the Marāṭhās took over exclusive control of the Parganā and strongly suggests that the granting of *aima* to Hindus was an established feature of the Niẓām's rule in the eighteenth century. Of the total number of grantees in this document, about 60 percent were Hindu names and 40 percent were Muslim names. Often the grants were only a *bīghā* or two of land, often half or more uncultivated. Most men held no specific offices. Equally suggestive of continuity between the Niẓām's administration and the Marāṭhās are documents from the period after the Marāṭhā conquest. For example, in 1751, of Adilabad Parganā's 106 cultivated villages, 16 were granted in *aima*, compared to 17 *aima* villages in the documents of the immediate per-conquest period of the late. The names are virtually identical (PK no. 194). This evidence of continuity is reinforced in Krishnaji Chitnis' (1994: 54–56) recent history of southern Maharashtra in the eighteenth century which discusses an *in'ām* grant of the *mullā* of a suburb of Dharwad. (The area had long been under the rule of Bijapur, and the *mullā* serviced the resident Muslim population.) Throughout the Marāṭhā period, the family retained a maintenance grant and continued its duties in the mosque. Like the grants we have considered in Adilabad, the only change was the levying of a small rent on the land of the grant, which had been entirely rent-free under the Mughuls. It is interesting that the form of this grant is identical to those of the village headman and the twelve 'village servants' (leatherworkers, carpenters, ironworkers, messengers) found throughout Maharashtra.

Let us now turn from Marāṭhā support of religious and learned Muslim men to the support of Muslim institutions. The evidence is equally clear. For example, the largest item in 'Miscellaneous expenses' in a year-end accounting of 1761 of Burhanpur was for the *dargāh* of Hazār Shāh Bhikhārī. The taxes to support this *dargāh* came from various *bāẓārs* within the city of Burhanpur (PK no. 198). At the same time, we find villages in Khandesh assigned for the maintenance of *dargāhs*. Consider, for example, in an account dated 1765:

> The following villages are continued in *in'ām* for maintenance of the *dargāh* of Shāhī Safū Nulā. Four villages in Zainpur Parganā [just outside Burhanpur], one in Raver, and one in Majrod [west into the hinterland of Burhanpur]. To these were added three in Zainpur and three in Majrod (PK no. 203; my translation).

Recent research has found similar practice in other areas of Maharashtra; for example, the Marāṭhās continued earlier Mughul grants of three *in'ām* villages in southern Maharashtra for the support of the *dargāh* of Jamāl Ṣāḥib and the *dargāh* of one Pīrzāda (Chitnis 1994: 134).

There is also strong evidence that grants for mosques continued under the Marāṭhās. Consider the following letter from the Peśvā to his local representative in the Tāptī Valley, in 1754:

> For the expenses of mosques, nine villages in Raver and Zainabad [two Parganās near Burhanpur] were given; these are to be continued as per the former Mughul government. A *sanad* is granted and given in accordance with Ṣalābat Juṅg (PK no. 198; my translation).[6]

To summarize, Marāṭhā administrative documents from the middle decades of the eighteenth century are quite detailed, allowing a relatively complete picture of government religious patronage of institutions and individuals both in the city of Burhanpur and the hinterland Parganās of Khandesh. From the Niẓām's control through the Marāṭhā conquest, there was a very high degree of continuity of patronage for both worthy Muslim men and Muslim institutions. This patronage was fully intermixed with that of worthy Hindus, a practice that seems to predate Marāṭhā control. The economic life of the city remained centered on Muslim weavers and Bohora Muslim traders who retained the tax advantages they established under Mughul rule.

DISJUNCTURES UNDER MARĀṬHĀ RULE OF BURHANPUR AND ITS HINTERLAND

The first change in the new Marāṭhā rule that greatly affected Muslims was in a tax called *zakāt*. Take, for example, the definitions from Horace Wilson's glossary of administrative and revenue terms:

> Zakāt. Alms, a contribution of a portion of income, obligatory on every Muslim possessed of capital. It is received by the *imām* and payable to the poor and needy.... The term literally signifying purification, is applied to *zakāt*; because the alms, etc. given sanctify the use of the remainder (1968: 656).

Compare this usage with the same term '*jakāt*' in a nineteenth-century Marathi dictionary: 'Jakāt. Customs or duties; land or transit duties' (Molesworth and Candy 1857: 301).

Throughout the period of the eighteenth century in the areas of northern Maharashtra and central India that I have studied, the Marāṭhās always collected *zakāt*. It appears as a significant tax in market towns, serai towns, large cities like Burhanpur, and rural areas producing for the cash market. Everywhere, the collection was just added to the general funds along with taxes on agriculture, for instance, and fines. Clearly, it was never allotted for maintenance of indigent virtuous Muslims, and the funds never reached the hands of the *imām*.

The second crucial change for Muslims in the Burhanpur area resulted from Marāṭhā military actions collectively termed 'seizing the Muglaī *'amal*s of the entire province of Khandesh.' Marāṭhā patrols captured, by force, all the estates on which mainly Muslim military grantees of the Niẓām were resident. Warfare raged up and down the hinterland of Burhanpur for a period of four years (1751–55). Villages became deserted as cultivators fled the fighting. Villages headmen and *deśmukh*s were imprisoned. By 1755, dozens of Muslim military leaders, large and small, had simply been displaced from their estates in the countryside around Burhanpur. Hundreds more had been displaced from the rest of the Khandesh Valley. Marāṭhā government transferred the grants to Marāṭhā generals.

For example, a letter of 1754 from the Peśvā to his official, Manājī Nikam, in the Parganā of Adilabad states:

> The Muglaī *'amal*s of the Parganās of Yedilabad [Adilabad] and Lohari have been granted to Jayājī Śinde as *jāgīr*. All collection after the subtraction of *sardeśmukhī*, *bābatī*, and expenses goes to him (PK no. 198; my translation).[7]

In no way can we minimize the effects that these seizures had on the support of Muslim culture in Burhanpur and its surrounding area. Under the Mughuls and the Niẓām, it had been private patronage, not government revenue, which built mosques, *madrasā*s (traditional schools), markets, and serais, dug wells and irrigation systems, planted trees, put up tombs and shrines, and laid out gardens. Any of these projects might be financed by a king but were equally likely built by nonroyal patrons with substantial landed income. This pattern prevailed throughout the Mughul Empire in the seventeenth century, just as it did at Burhanpur.[8] In the middle years of the eighteenth century the military class capable of private support for this infrastructure was simply displaced from the areas surrounding Burhanpur.

It is important to note, however, that this displacement was not religiously based. The many Hindu Rājpūt military grantees in the area were displaced with the same vigor and thoroughness as the Muslim grantees. The matter was one of state and military control; the Marāṭhās simply could not leave heavily armed units residing in the countryside and have any hopes of establishing credible peace and tax collection.

In addition to the Niẓām's military elite, the upper-tax-collecting bureaucracy was also displaced. For thirty years prior to 1751, the Marāṭhās and the Niẓām had shared the revenue from Khandesh, the hinterland of Burhanpur. Each collected their share of the taxes. When the Marāṭhās took over the province, we do not find the Niẓām's tax collectors reappearing in Marāṭhā service. In the whole of Khandesh province, all of the tax collectors of the second half of the eighteenth century were Maharashtrian or Koṅkaṇastha Brāhmaṇa. Thus, a second crucial group of private Muslim patrons in Khandesh was no longer able to provide support for infrastructure and institutions.

This process is paralleled exactly in the area of southern Maharashtra studied by Chitnis. Like my area of Khandesh, Chitnis (1994: 134–35) finds that the most important change from Muslim rule to Marāṭhā rule was the disappearance of Muslim military grants and the replacement of Muslim tax collecting officials by Brāhmaṇas in service of the Marāṭhā government.

I would like to emphasize two points that I find crucial to this process. First, I am not suggesting that infrastructure ceased to be built after the Marāṭhās took over the area around Burhanpur. Quite to the contrary, irrigation systems, town markets, and serais were built. I have traced this process at some length elsewhere (Gordon 1994: Chapter 5). It was simply a different group of grantees and officials who built them: mainly Marāṭhās and Brāhmaṇas. This group no longer supported specifically Muslim institutions (*madrasās*, mosques) with private donations.

Second, we cannot view these displacements as religiously motivated—somehow a 'Hindu' state displacing the elite of a 'Muslim' state. The process was the same in every detail when the Marāṭhās conquered a Hindu area. For example, in the 1750s, when the Marāṭhā generals, Śinde and Hoḷkar, attacked the Jāṭ kingdom south of Agra, they made every attempt to displace local militarized groups in the countryside. All were Hindus. Likewise, the Marāṭhās displaced the existing tax collectors (Brāhmaṇas mostly) and assigned collectors of their own (likewise Brāhmaṇas). A decade later, the Marāṭhās attacked Rājpūt states with the same general pattern. Conquest and state control were the goals; religion was no issue. All involved were Hindus. This process of displacement of tax collecting officials and replacement of countryside-based militarized elites was what conquest meant in the eighteenth century. The process had a long tradition, certainly predating the Mughuls.[9]

CONCLUSIONS

Overall, there is almost no sense in which we can treat the Marāṭhā state as Hindu, nor Hindu and Muslim as other, within the Marāṭhā polity. Rather than a Hindu state operating solely on the basis of *dharma* as interpreted by Brāhmaṇas, we are, I believe, seeing three competing systems of legitimacy, side by side, none decisively dominant. The first, indeed, was a vision of the dharmic king. In this conception, the foremost responsibility of a ruler was the protection of gods, Brāhmaṇas, and cows. Any ruler who failed in these duties had no claim to legitimate rule. This position was laid out in the *Ajñapatra*, a mirror-of-princes Marathi text written for Śivājī's successors in the late seventeenth century, but much more strongly in other texts of the period, such as the *Śivabhārata* or the writings of Rāmadāsa. The failure of Muslim rulers to fulfill these kingly duties was the basis for demonizing them in these texts.

Nevertheless, a second entire conception of legitimacy came to the Marāṭhās as warrior families in the Deccan. As direct heirs to both the Deccan Sulṭāns and, later, Mughul rule, Marāṭhās' sense of honor, even their sense of differentiation from Kuṇbī cultivators, was completely enmeshed with service to the Deccan Sulṭāns. Even Śivājī, we should recall, though he disdained active Bijapuri service, became a Mughul *manṣabdār* and took part in active Mughul service. Material reward for such service, whether with Bijapur or the Mughuls, consisted of a series of *in'āms* or *sanads*, granting government's share of tax revenue in a home area (a *waṭan* or a *waṭan jāgīr*). In court cases of disputed local rights, possession of a properly signed, sealed *sanad* was the strongest piece of evidence a family could bring before any Marāṭhā court. This legitimacy by *sanad* was, if anything, stronger in the eighteenth century than in the seventeenth century. In the carefully worded treaty of 1721, for example, the Marāṭhās took seriously their rights to Mughul authority as *nā'ibṣūbadārs* of the Deccan.

At the practical level, this concern with precedent and established rights lends an intensely conservative flavor to Marāṭhā administration. In practice, the legitimacy of precedent seems at least as strong as the legitimacy of fulfilling the dharmic duties of Hindu kingship. Consider this letter from the Peśvā to Śaṅkrājī Nikam, his representative in eastern Malwa:

> From the Parganā Sironj to Burhanpur elephants and camels carry goods. The cess should be taken only at Sironj and not at Burhanpur. ... It is understood that you are not taking the cess at Sironj but double at Burhanpur. Why so? You should act according to the old custom and no new rules should be promulgated.

Both of these notions of legitimacy were competing with yet a third conception, that of universal kingship. The overall tone of the *Ajñapatra*, for example, is that a king must be pragmatic in order to rule. His legitimacy came neither strictly from a *dharmaśāstra* nor from a *sanad* but from promoting peace and prosperity among all his subjects. The *Ajñapatra* is, on the whole, a rather Machiavellian document that deals with ways to control the kings own military nobility, the construction and stocking of forts, and the delicate relation between kings and ministers. It is interesting that the only groups that the *Ajñapatra*'s author singled out for caution were those he perceived to be a direct threat to the state—the Siddis of Janjira, Awrangzīb's forces, and European merchants.[10] Nowhere in the work were Muslims as a whole treated as a group. Rather, it was assumed that they, like all other groups, would benefit from a vigilant, resourceful king.

Overall in the Marāṭhā kingdom, there seems to have been, in the seventeenth and the eighteenth centuries, a constant tension between rhetoric and policy which centered on these three competing systems of legitimacy.[11] We must envision constant dialogue within the ruling elite—both Marāṭhās and Brāhmaṇas—on policy and strategy. The documents that remain, produced entirely by Brāhmaṇas, reflect a whole range of sentiment, from fiercely anti-Muslim to consciously allying with Muslim powers.

The conception of 'other,' thus, seems entirely inadequate to deal with the situation of eighteenth-century India. Neither Hindus nor Muslims defined themselves by what the other was not. Unlike the truly divided world of seventeenth-century Europe, Muslims and Hindus wore the same clothes, took service in the same armies, allied across religious lines, and formed trade and credit networks spanning both sorts of states. In a close examination of a region that passed from 'Muslim' rule to 'Hindu' rule, we have seen relatively little change. Mosques and Muslim holy men continued to be supported, Muslim *deśmukhs* were just as legitimately the 'mouth of the land' as Hindus in nearby areas. If anything, the conservative nature of Marāṭhā rule favored Muslim traders by retaining the tax advantages that had been set under the Mughul Empire. Bohora Muslims, thus, remained the dominant trading group in Burhanpur.

Where the structure of patronage radically changed was in the area of private donations. None of these three systems of legitimacy prevented the invading Marāṭhās from displacing the Niẓām's military and bureaucratic elite, both Muslim and Rājpūt from Burhanpur and Khandesh. The new Brāhmaṇa officials and Marāṭhā generals shifted patronage to the channels they knew. Rāmacandra Bābā, for example, was a Koṅkaṇastha Brāhmaṇa who prospered in the Peśvā's service in north of Burhanpur; he used his new wealth to build and endow a large temple in his native Goa (Sunṭaṇkara 1973). In the wider sphere of eighteenth-century India, the Marāṭhās—by control of the 'Muglaī *'amals*'—replaced Rājpūts as the largest patrons of *ghāṭs* (river banks), rest houses, and temples at Benares and other major temple sites throughout India.

Finally, let us return to the larger concerns raised at the opening of the chapter. It did not take long for the European world of the seventeenth century to divide along religious lines. In slightly over one generation politics, army recruitment, dress, trade networks, and military alliances divided between 'Catholic' and 'Protestant.' There is no doubt that the issues—Church luxury, Church intercession versus a personal relation to God, corruption of priests, local versus papal authority—had been building for generations. Nevertheless, the creation of 'other' happened quite quickly. I think that this is useful in understanding relations between Muslims and Hindus in India. It is simply not necessary or useful to project the current animosity backward into ancient, immutable divides of 'otherness.' These divides can happen quite quickly; we need only look at today's tragedies in Rwanda or the former Yugoslavia to see the rapidity of development of ethnic and religious hatred and conflict. In the case of India, it seems much more productive to look to the politics of the twentieth century, both the reluctance of the Congress party to recognize representation of minorities and especially the memories of the violence of partition, for the roots of the current religious politics.

The theoretical work of Otnes suggests how this analysis might begin. Recall that Otnes gives primacy to a triadic relationship; relations between people (the two outer ends of the triad) are always mediated by a central socially constructed 'object'—a contract, a cow, a building, a cooking pot, a martyr. Defining a relation to this object is crucial to understanding the relation of the two persons (or groups) to each other. It is suggestive that in the case of seventeenth-century Europe, there was a rapid erasure of common definitions of these socially constructed 'objects'—a church, the meaning of dress, contracts. Because 'Catholics' and 'Protestants' were defining intervening objects radically differently, relationships between the two groups withered, and they became 'other.' This may be a useful way to analyze many situations of alterity, including the current-day development of Hindu-Muslim animosity in India.

Notes

1. Even older Chinese literature described nomadic groups beyond the wall as other in similar terms.

2. Any state will do as an example. In the 1730s the Marāṭhā conquest of Muslim Bhopal differed in no way from the conquest of Hindu Bhilsa, immediately to the north. In the 1750s, the Marāṭhās eagerly sought an alliance with Muslim Oude against the Muslim Afghan invader. Hindu Marāṭhās fought Hindu Rājpūts and Hindu Jāṭs throughout the 1780s.

3. For the terms of the treaty, see SPD n.s. 1, selection 149, also 155.

4. The SPD details cash grants for celebration of both Hindu festivals and ceremonies for Muslim saints.

5. *Ṭakās* and *rukh*s were a copper currency of account at this time, though silver rupees were more commonly used in actual collection.

6. A similar grant has been published in SPD (45, selection 101). It is an *in'ām*

for the lamps of a mosque.

7. See for comparison the analysis of the distribution of the *jāgīrdār* estate in Kate (1987: 92–93).

8. The well-known Urdu couplet suggests: 'He is not dead who leaves behind him on earth bridge and mosque, well and serai' (cited in Blake 1991: 69).

9. In the late seventeenth century, for example, Marāṭhās knew that the Mughuls had failed in Maharashtra when they failed to displace Marāṭhā militarized families or successfully substitute their own tax collectors.

10. Because the Europeans were, unlike other merchants, 'representatives of kings.'

11. One could also conceptualize this process as tension between a vernacular (Marathi) and two different cosmopolitan systems (Persian and Sanskrit) (see Pollock 1999).

References Cited

Bhabha, Homi. 1990. *Nation and Narration*. London: Routledge.

Blake, Stephen P. 1991. *Shahjahanabad: The Sovereign City in Mughal India, 1639–1739*. Cambridge: Cambridge University Press.

Buber, Martin. 1958 [1922]. *I and Thou* (trans. Ronald Gregor Smith). New York: Charles Scribner.

Chitnis, K. N. 1994. *Glimpses of Maratha Socio-Economic History*. New Delhi: Atlantic.

Corbey, Raymond, and Joseph Th. Leersen. 1991. *Alterity, Identity, and Image: Selves and Others in Society and Scholarship*. Amsterdam: Rodopi.

Dostal, Robert J. 1997. "The End of Metaphysics and the Possibility of Non-Hegelian Speculative Thought." *In* Shaun Gallagher, ed., *Hegel, History, and Interpretation*, 33–42. New York: State University of New York Press.

Dunn, Richard S. 1970. *The Age of Religious Wars, 1559–1689*. New York: Norton.

Fabian, Johannes. 1983. *Time and the Other: How Anthropology Makes Its Object*. New York: Columbia University Press.

Fanon, Frantz. 1963 [1961]. *The Wretched of the Earth* (trans. Constance Farrington). New York: Grove Press.

Forster, E. M. 1924. *A Passage to India*. New York: Harcourt, Brace.

Foucault, Michel. 1965 [1961]. *Madness and Civilization: A History of Insanity in the Age of Reason* (trans. Richard Howard). New York: Pantheon.

Geertz, Clifford. 1988. *Work and Lives: The Anthropologist as Author*. Stanford: Stanford University Press.

Gordon, Stewart. 1994. *Marathas, Marauders, and State-Formation in Eight-*

eenth-Century India. Delhi: Oxford University Press.

Gramsci, Antonio. 1992. *Prison Notebooks* (trans. Joseph A. Buttigieg and Antonio Callari). 2 vols. New York: Columbia University Press.

Harrington, Michael. 1962. *Other America: Poverty in the United States*. New York: Macmillan.

Harris, H. S. 1997. "The Hegelian Organon of Interpretation." *In* Shaun Gallagher, ed., *Hegel, History, and Interpretation*, 19–31. New York: State University of New York Press.

Hartog, François. 1988 [1980]. *The Mirror of Herodotus: The Representation of the Other in the Writing of History* (trans. Janet Lloyd). Berkeley: University of California Press.

Heidegger, Martin. 1949 [1929–43]. *Existence and Being* (trans. Douglas Scott, chapters 1 and 2; R. F. C. Hull and Alan Crich, chapters 3 and 4). Chicago: Henry Regnery.

Hughes, Christopher. 1974. *Switzerland*. New York: Praeger.

Inden, Ronald. 1990. *Imagining India*. Oxford: Basil Blackwell.

Kant, Immanuel. 1929 [1781]. *Critique of Pure Reason* (trans. Norman Kemp Smith). London: Macmillan.

Kate, P. V. 1987. *Marathwada Under the Nizams, 1724–1948*. Delhi: Mittal Publications.

Klemm, David E., and Gunter Zoller, eds. 1969. *Figuring the Self: Subject, Absolute, and Others in Classical German Philosophy*. Albany: State University of New York Press.

Maland, David. 1980. *Europe at War: 1600–1650*. Lanham: Rowman & Littlefield.

Marcuse, Herbert. 1954 [1941]. *Reason and Revolution: Hegel and the Rise of Social Theory*. New York: Humanities Press.

Molesworth, J. T., assisted by George Candy and Thomas Candy. 1857. *A Dictionary: Maráthí and English*. Bombay: Bombay Education Society's Press.

Munck, Thomas. 1990. *Seventeenth-Century Europe: State, Conflict, and the Social Order in Europe 1598–1700*. Basingstoke: Macmillan.

Otnes, Per. 1997. *Other-wise: Alterity, Materiality, Mediation*. Oslo: Scandinavian University Press.

PK [Peśvā Khaṇḍeś Collection]. Puṇe daftar, Pune, India.

Polisensky, J. V. 1971 [1968]. *The Thirty Years' War* (trans. Robert Evens). Berkeley: University of California Press.

Pollock, Sheldon. 1999. "The Cultural Vernacular." *Journal of Asian Studies* 58, 1: 6–38.

Said, Edward. 1978. *Orientalism*. New York: Random.

Sartre, Jean-Paul. 1957 [1943]. *Being and Nothingness: An Essay on Phenome-*

nological Ontology (trans. Hazel E. Barnes). London: Methuen.

SPD. 1930–34. *Selections from the Peśvā daftar*. 45 vols. Mumbai: Government Central Press.

SPD n.s. 1952–57. *Selections from the Peśvā daftar, New Series*. 7 vols. Mumbai: Government Central Press.

SSRPD. 1906–11. *Selections from the Satara Raja's and the Peishwa Diaries* (eds. G. C. Vad, P. V. Mawjee, and D. B. Parasnis). 9 vols. Poona: Deccan Vernacular Translation Society.

Sunṭaṇkara, Śāntārāma. 1973. *Aśi āhe Śrīśāntādurgā*. Belagāṁva: Jijñāsā Prakāśana.

Wilson, H. H. 1968 [1855]. *A Glossary of Judicial and Revenue Terms*. Delhi: Munshiram Manoharlal.

Fortuitous Convergences and Essential Ambiguities: Transcultural Political Elites in the Medieval Deccan

Phillip B. Wagoner

It is virtually axiomatic that 'Hindu' and 'Muslim' are fundamental and inescapable categories of identity in modern South Asia and that each is in large measure constituted in opposition to its other.[1] Yet there is an abundance of evidence dating from the premodern period that suggests that this was not always the case. To judge from epigraphic data, the medieval Deccan was one historical milieu in which the religious categories 'Hindu' and 'Muslim' appear to have been of minimal relevance as primary bases of identity. Instead, as Cynthia Talbot (1995) has shown, identity was more likely to be cast in ethnic rather than religious terms, with designations such as 'Turuṣka,' 'Pārasīka,' 'Telugu,' 'Karnāṭa,' and 'Oṛiyā' figuring in inscriptions more frequently than 'Muslim' or 'Hindu.' Following this epigraphic cue, one might reasonably decide to avoid religious labels in discussing individual identity; but, even so, one may still wish to distinguish analytically between the broader cultural traditions to which individuals belong. Accordingly, one could then speak of the 'Indic' languages, patterns of dress, systems of food, and other cultural practices that were favored by Telugus, Karnatas, and Oriyas, in contrast to the 'Islamicate' traditions followed by Turushkas and Parasikas. But even here things are not quite as clear-cut as they may seem, since 'Indic' cultural forms and practices in the Deccan were often heavily 'Islamicized' and vice versa. At Vijayanagara, for example, men of the ruling elite dressed in public in an Arab-style tunic known in the local vernaculars as *kabāyi* (from the Arab *qabā'*; Wagoner 1996), while Ibrāhīm 'Ādil Shāh II, one of the best known rulers of the neighboring kingdom of Bijapur, is remembered as the author of the *Kitāb-i Nauras* (from the Sanskrit *navarasa,* 'nine aesthetic moods'), an important Persian work dealing with classical Sanskrit *rasa* theory and written in a heavily

Sanskritized vocabulary (Eaton 1978: 98ff.).

What truly complicates matters, however, is the data pertaining to the cultural and social practices of individual human beings in the medieval Deccan, for whom cultural code switching and boundary crossing seem to have been familiar parts of everyday life. Indeed, as soon as historical records are examined, one sees how problematic it is to understand premodern Deccani society in terms of communally defined categories—whether through the application of explicitly religious labels ('Hindu' and 'Muslim') or in the more subtle guise of their secularized cultural counterparts ('Indic' and 'Islamicate'). In this chapter, I would like to consider the actions of two individuals for whom we have some such documentation, in the hope that their examples might begin to suggest both the fluid nature of individual identity and the permeability of cultural boundaries in the premodern Deccan.

AN 'OFFICER OF DISTINCTION': THE CASE OF 'AIN AL-MULK GĪLĀNI

Let us begin by considering the career of one 'Ain al-Mulk Gīlāni, a prominent military and political figure who flourished throughout the second half of the sixteenth century. The sources that are available for this figure are varied and include the early seventeenth-century *Tārīkh-i Firishta* (History of Firishta), written in Persian at Bijapur under 'Ādil Shāhī patronage; the late sixteenth-century *Rāyavācakamu*, an anonymous historiographic text in Telugu written at the Nāyaka court of Madurai; and at least two Sanskrit inscriptions issued in 'Ain al-Mulk's lifetime and referring to his donative activity. Although the *Tārīkh-i Firishta* is the latest of our sources and bears the status of a subsequent historiographic representation rather than a contemporary document, we may well begin with it given the coherence and detail of its narrative of 'Ain al-Mulk's career.[2]

Sometime about 1542, according to Firishta, 'Ain al-Mulk Gīlāni entered the service of Ibrāhīm 'Ādil Shāh I of Bijapur after having been lured away from an earlier relationship with the declining Bahmānī kingdom. He is said to have been attracted to the 'Ādil Shāhī cause through the efforts of the Bijapuri minister, Asad Khān, and was rewarded with the estates of another officer, Yūsuf Turk, who had just fallen from favor (Firishta 1966, 3: 54–55). Firishta goes on to report that by 1550 'Ain al-Mulk had offended the 'Ādil Shāh and left his service together with his force of some four thousand cavalry to enter that of the Vijayanagara ruler Aravīṭ Rāma Rāja (also known as Rāmarāya). Firishta adds that ' 'Ain al-Mulk had on many occasions so distinguished himself by his bravery that the Rāja used to call him brother' (Firishta 1966, 3: 229). It appears that 'Ain al-Mulk was still in Rāma Rāja's service in the late 1550s and early 1560s, since Firishta notes that he was one of the leaders of a joint expedition of Vijayanagara and Bijapuri forces against Golconda that occurred at some point between 1557 and 1565 (Firishta 1966, 3: 244–45). This is apparently the last reference to 'Ain al-Mulk during the Vijayanagara phase of his career; Firishta does not mention his name in the account he gives of the fateful battle of Talikot (1565), in which Vijayanagara power was decisively broken by the combined forces of the northern Deccani Sulṭānates and Rāma Rāja was captured and beheaded.

Some fifteen or twenty years later, however, 'Ain al-Mulk appears back in Bijapur, where, according to Firishta, he played a major role as a power broker in the struggles between a succession of would-be regents for the young Ibrāhīm 'Ādil Shāh II (who had acceded to the throne at the age of nine in 1579) (Firishta 1966, 3: 87–101, *passim*). In 1590, he helped Ibrāhīm II take the throne for himself by ousting the regent Dilāwar Khān, and as a reward for this service, he was presented with robes of honor (Firishta 1966, 3: 101–3). Three years later, however, he turned against his ruler and conspired with Ibrāhīm's brother Ismā'īl, who had set up the standard of revolt from the fort at Belgaum. But Ibrāhīm 'Ādil Shāh managed to retain the upper hand throughout this incident, and 'Ain al-Mulk was slain in battle. Firishta closes his account of 'Ain al-Mulk Gīlānī's final chapter with a gruesome account of the rewards of his treachery, noting that Ibrāhīm 'Ādil Shāh had the traitor's head impaled on a pole before the main gate of the palace. Afterward, he had it 'put into a great gun' whence it was blown into the air 'so that no traces might remain of it' (Firishta 1966, 3: 103–111).

One might be inclined to dismiss Firishta's claim that 'Ain al-Mulk actually entered the service of Vijayanagara were it not for the corroborating testimony provided by contemporary documents. In 1551, 'Ain al-Mulk's position within the Vijayanagara state is confirmed by what may, upon first consideration, appear to be an unexpected source: a Sanskrit copper plate inscription from Bevinahaḷḷi in Raichur District, recording an *agrahāram* grant made by the Vijayanagara king Sadāśivarāya at 'Ain al-Mulk's request (EI 14, no. 16).[3] In these plates 'Ainanamalukka'—as his name is recorded in Sanskrit—appears in the role of a *vijñāpti* (petitioner), requesting his Vijayanagara overlord to make a gift of lands to a group of eighty Brāhmaṇas (each one individually identified by name, *gotra* [clan], and *śākhā* [school of Vedic recitation] to which he belongs). Although the rhetoric of the epigraph portrays the *de jure* reigning king Sadāśivarāya as the donor of the lands and the minister and *de facto* ruler Aravīṭ Rāma Rāja as the *vijñāpti*, it is still clear in identifying Ainanamalukka as the ultimate instigator of the donation. Thus, when the 'honorable great king

Sadāśiva poured a stream of gold and water and happily made the donation to those wise ones,' he is stated to have been 'following the request of the heroic Rāma Rāja' (EI 14, no. 16, lines 126–30; my translation); but then Rāma Rāja himself is described as 'having been entreated by the jewel of the Kanyārna family, the hero Ainanamalukka—a veritable wish-fulfilling tree for our earth, born as the fruit of previous good works done by [his father] Prauḍha Ainanamalukkendra, and a conqueror of enemy kings—who had joined his hands together in respectful obeisance' (EI 14, no. 16, lines 122–25; my translation). The formulation may appear complex, but the epigraph in fact follows a well-established convention governing donative activity that can be seen in countless grants involving the gifting of land within a system of feudal tenure (Sircar 1965: 114ff.). The clear implication here is that the lands in question lay within the estate (*sīmā, amaraṃ*) of Ainanamalukka, who, in return for providing military service to the Vijayanagara throne, enjoyed rights to the productive yield of the land but did not possess the right to alienate that land without first securing the approval of the king as its legal owner. Thus, we must recognize that although the inscription correctly represents the shadowy Sadāśivarāya as the *legal* donor of this *agrahāram* grant, the *real* donor—in the sense of the individual who actually alienates something of value (his claim to collect revenue) and takes the initiative to arrange for the transaction—is none other than Ainanamalukka, whose munificence is underscored through the inscription's characterization of him as 'a wish-fulfilling tree for our earth.' By acting as a *vijñāpti*, he was defining himself both as a powerful agent controlling the productive resources of the land within his estate and, simultaneously, as a subordinate member within a hierarchy of authority, linking him through the person of Aravīṭ Rāma Rāja to the Vijayanagara emperor himself.[4]

Interestingly, 'Ain al-Mulk's memory was perpetuated not only in the pages of Firishta's Persian history but also in another historiographic text, the Telugu *Rāyavācakamu*, written anonymously in Madurai in the closing years of the sixteenth century, in which he prominently figures. In this account, 'Ain al-Mulk—here called 'Ayyanamalaka'—figures as a paragon of loyal service to Vijayanagara, even though his previous service at Bijapur is openly acknowledged (Wagoner 1993: 122). In this text, we find 'Ain al-Mulk heading the list of the 'Sons of the Eating Dish' (*harivāṇaṃ komāḷḷu*), a class of honored retainers who are fictively adopted as the king's sons. Even more significant is the fact that the author of the *Rāyavācakamu* casts 'Ain al-Mulk as an authority on the prior history of the northern Deccani kingdoms and uses him as a mouthpiece for a long disquisition on the cultural and moral shortcomings of the 'Turks,' that is, the ruling elite of the kingdoms of Bijapur, Ahmadnagar, and Golconda. Thus when the Vijayanagara king Kṛṣṇadevarāya asks 'Ain al-Mulk to explain the circumstances surrounding the rise to power of these Turk rulers, he not only satisfies the king's demand but also continues by dismissing the king's fears that they pose any serious military threat:

> You see, my lord, when the Turks set out for the battlefront, they don't proceed cautiously, gauging themselves with the opposing force. Instead, they just advance obstinately. If it so happens that they outnumber and defeat the opposing force, then, no matter how fast the other soldiers flee, the Turks will keep coming and massacring them. If, on the other hand, the opposing force stands firm, then they beg their commanders to let them go back. When the strategists back at the palace get word of this, they decide that fighting is not the right thing to do under the circumstances, so they order the forces to be recalled, and you can be sure that those men retreat as fast as they can. And, believe it or not, when the message that they should return reaches the battlefront, they don't even stop to consider the disgrace that they will cause their ruler by retreating. The people of Karnataka, on the other hand, they have the power of discrimination; they know the difference between what can be done and what cannot. Once the decision has been made to fight, then, even if all seems hopeless, in the thick of battle you do not lose your resolve. With a clear conscience you can go ahead and order your men to march forward and meet the foe, and all those foot soldiers will rise bravely to the task because yours is the power of a real master (Wagoner 1993: 124).

Evidently, 'Ain al-Mulk had become so thoroughly 'naturalized' in South Indian historical memory, that it did not appear inherently ironic or problematic that he should be cast in this role as a consummate Vijayanagara 'insider.' If Ayyanamalaka is made to articulate a cultural polemic deriding the Turks and their conduct in battle while holding up the ideal of the 'people of Karnataka,' the author of this text clearly sees him as a member of the latter group and not of the alien ethnic group he is deriding. At the same time, however, the text's representation of 'Ain al-Mulk includes an element of ambiguity in his identity —not because of religion but by virtue of his prior service at Bijapur—that is essential to his social functioning, singling him out as the one person who can speak with authority about the military tactics of the Turks.

Considering these varied sources relating to 'Ain al-Mulk, what conclusions can we draw about the bases of social identity and the nature of cultural boundaries in the medieval Deccan? First, we must register the fact that 'Ain al-Mulk is identified not in terms of religious categories but in terms of his membership in an elite social class. Neither Firishta, nor the author of the Bevinahaḷḷi grant, nor the anonymous author of the *Rāyavācakamu*, ever characterizes 'Ain al-Mulk as a Muslim or uses any comparable religiously defined term to refer to him; nor is he represented in any of the available sources as performing any actions or espousing any beliefs or attitudes which might be considered to be characteristically 'Islamic.' In fact, the closest he comes to being represented as engaged in 'religious' activity of any sort is when he is identified in the Bevinahaḷḷi inscription as the instigator of the *agrahāram* grant it records and is, thus, represented as the munificent supporter of eighty Brāhmaṇas and of the village's deities Śiva and Viṣṇu. All this is in striking contrast to the way 'Ain al-Mulk has been characterized by scholars writing in the twentieth century, who have, without exception, characterized him as a Muslim, presumably on the sole basis of the Perso-Arabic form of his name. Thus, S. V. Venkateswara and S. V. Viswanathan, the editors of the Bevinahaḷḷi grant, identify him as 'A Muhammadan subordinate chieftain under Sadasivaraya' (EI 14: 211); C. Hayavadana Rao, prefacing his brief discussion of 'Ain al-Mulk, states that 'Rāma Rāja appears to have encouraged the entertainment in his service of Muhammadans' (1930: 2110); and, I myself, in a note to my translation of the *Rāyavācakamu*, have characterized him as 'A Muslim warrior who left Bijapur to take up service at Vijayanagara' (Wagoner 1993: 203n16). What is at issue here is not whether 'Ain al-Mulk was a Muslim but the profound difference in cognitive stance between those who wrote about him in the sixteenth and seventeenth centuries and those who have interpreted those writings in the twentieth century. However fundamental communally defined categories may be in our own day, we must recognize that for 'Ain al-Mulk's contemporaries—at least for those who moved within the same social spaces—an individual's particular religious affiliation and leanings appear to have been matters of little interest.

What *was* important in the sixteenth century was whether an individual belonged to a particular elite social class, one that was defined in terms of the mastery of military skills, the acceptance of specific notions of lordship and service, and the ability to command economic and social resources. This emphasis is as evident in Firishta's portrayal of 'Ain al-Mulk as it is in the *Rāyavācakamu*. Thus, for Firishta, 'Ain al-Mulk is not a 'Muslim' but an 'officer of distinction,' and the narrative of his career revolves around his military exploits, his shifting political alliances, and the changing nature of his relationship with the various rulers he serves in succession. Similarly, from the perspective of the author of the *Rāyavācakamu*, 'Ain al-Mulk is identified not with reference to his religious affiliation but in terms of his social identity and membership within an elite group of retainers who are fictively adopted as the king's sons (note the intriguing resonance with Firishta's statement that the king 'used to call him "brother" '). And even in the Bevinahaḷḷi grant, in which religious actions may appear to be most clearly in evidence, 'Ain al-Mulk is never identified in religious terms but only in terms of his membership in a particular lineage (the 'Kanyārna *kula*') and with reference to his martial exploits (he is the 'hero' and a 'conqueror of enemy kings') and his exceptional liberality in redistributing the wealth he commands, making him a 'wish-fulfilling tree for our earth.'

The second point suggested by our evidence concerns the cultural parameters of the elite military-political class to which 'Ain al-Mulk belonged. This class was not divided into separate 'Hindu' and 'Muslim' segments but constituted a single transcultural social formation, one that transcended and cut across the boundaries that are generally understood to have divided the medieval Deccan into distinct Indic and Islamicate cultural spheres. This is suggested not only by the apparent ease with which 'Ain al-Mulk migrates back and forth between Indic and Islamicate states but also by the fact that none of the sources signal this movement as being unusual or out of the ordinary in any way. Indeed, there are numerous other documented instances of members of this overarching military-political elite moving back and forth across the presumed Indic-Islamicate cultural divide. Thus, Firishta notes that Rāma Rāja himself began his career as an Iqṭā'dār in the service of the Golconda court, before transferring his loyalties to the Vijayanagara state. The *Rāyavācakamu* identifies two of 'Ain al-Mulk's cohorts within the elite corps known as the 'Sons of the Eating Dish'—namely Aṃkuśa Rāvu (also known as Aṃkuśa Khān) and Rāṇā Jagadeva—as likewise having earlier served at Bijapur, a suggestion that is in essence corroborated by other contemporary historical sources (see Wagoner 1993: 122, 124, 204n16; although this evidence suggests that these two figures served not Bijapur but Golconda and the 'Imād Shāhīs at Berar). Historically, this class would appear to have been formed through a process of social convergence between indigenous Indic military elites and the immigrant Perso-Turkic elite that arrived in the Deccan in the thirteenth century with the southward expansion of the Delhi Sulṭānate. As members of these two elites moved within a common sphere of interaction along the shifting Deccan frontier, competing for control of the same economic and social resources, and engaging alternately in conflicts and alliances, they would increasingly have exchanged elements of their respective cultures until they were soon using a common assemblage of instruments and techniques to achieve social and economic domination (mounted archery, forms of landholding, use of paper and pen for record keeping). Certainly by the sixteenth century, if not in the fifteenth century or even before, this convergence had progressed far enough that we can meaningfully speak of a single, transcultural military-political elite, multiethnic and multilingual in composition but united through shared bodies of material culture and common social interests.

While the evidence suggests that the common political and military culture shared by the members of this class gave them great mobility and enabled them to function effectively within any state along the Deccan frontier, this should not obscure the fact that there remained significant cultural differences between these states. These differences hinged upon the particular languages, religious practices, and ideological systems that dominated the public sphere at a given court. Bijapur and Vijayanagara might both have shared the common name of 'City of Victory,' but at the Islamicate City of Victory the primary languages of the court were Dakhni and Persian.[5] Islamic religious practices were dominant; and state power was legitimated by the religious authority held by prominent Ṣūfī *shaykhs* and the scholarly *'ulamā'*. At its Indic counterpart, on the other hand, Kannada, Telugu, and Sanskrit were the primary court languages. Hindu ritual practices were predominant; and the ruler was legitimated by the authority manifested by Hindu deities and Brāhmaṇa ritual specialists. In order to negotiate cultural differences such as these, individual members of this political-military elite would have needed proficiency in multiple languages and cultural codes, and they would have had to know how and when to switch between them effectively. Clearly, men like 'Ain al-Mulk and Aravīṭ Rāma Rāja could not have migrated successfully between the predominantly Islamicate world of Bijapur and Golconda and the more Indic world of Vijayanagara had they not been proficient in Telugu or Kannada as well as in Dakhni or Persian. Indeed, the evidence of historical linguistics suggests that it would have been common for members of the military-political elite to possess competence in several languages, not just within the 'Indic' group (Telugu, Kannada, Sanskrit) or within the 'Islamicate' group (Dakhni, Persian, Arabic) but, more to the point, in languages that cut across these culturally defined groupings. This is evident from the significant numbers of Persian and Arabic loan words in later medieval Telugu—some two hundred are recorded in inscriptions beginning in the latter half of the fifteenth century, and some nine hundred are attested in literary works. Significantly, most of these loan words occur in areas of the lexicon relating to politics (*sultānu, pāduṣā, pharmānā, hujūru*), warfare (*sipāyī, tupākī, phirāyiṃcu*), and revenue administration (*kaulu, kuśkī, dumbālā, kāgitam, kalam*)—the very aspects of social life that were dominated by this elite military-political class (Svarājyalakṣmī 1979: 330). Moving from the other direction, the lexical characteristics of Dakhni similarly point to a significant degree of bilingualism. In contrast to North Indian Urdu, medieval Dakhni Urdu not only tends to use much less Arabic and Persian vocabulary but also shows evidence of having absorbed a large Sanskritic vocabulary, presumably brought in through the medium of Telugu and Kannada loan words (Eaton 1978: 92).[6]

But above and beyond the literal linguistic level, members of the transcultural military-political elite would also have been required to switch between the different cultural codes that were employed in Indic and Islamicate courtly settings. In order to negotiate successfully between these dominant cultural codes, it would have been necessary for the members of this elite to make judgments about the functional or situational commensurability of the coded acts in question. Had ʿAin al-Mulk been interested in demonstrating his liberality at Bijapur, he might have done so by endowing a Ṣūfī *dargāh* (shrine) or some comparable Islamic institution; but in order to express his liberality during the Vijayanagara phase of his career—and to do so in terms that would simultaneously situate him clearly within the Vijayanagara political hierarchy—he chose not to endow a *dargāh* but to perform such a quintessentially 'Hindu' act of patronage as establishing an *agrahāram* village for the maintenance of learned Brāhmaṇas. Such a decision implies the operation of an underlying cultural hermeneutic, that is, an act of interpretation in which the specific signs and practices of one culture are understood in the terms of another. In this particular case, the judgment implicit in ʿAin al-Mulk's act is that, within an Indic context, the patronage of *agrahāram* villages is analogous to the patronage of *dargāhs* and comparable charitable institutions in an Islamicate context. In other words, the *agrahāram* is defined not as some Hindu 'other' of the Muslim's *dargāh* but in terms of its broad social and cultural equivalence with the Islamic institution.[7]

AḤMAD KHĀN'S 'DHARMASĀLE'

The next case I would like to discuss is of interest because it sheds light on the actual workings of this hermeneutic operation. Specifically, this case calls attention to the social dimensions of the process through which commensurability is negotiated, attesting to the collaborative nature of the enterprise. The case revolves around the construction of a religious edifice in the Vijayanagara capital in 1439 and the commemoration of this act in a brief Kannada epigraph inscribed over the building's entrance. To begin with, what is of particular interest here is the series of apparently contradictory signals that are generated by this building and its inscription. In terms of its liturgical space, the edifice is clearly recognizable as a mosque, but stylistically, it is realized through the architectural forms typical of the familiar Indic *maṇḍapa* (pillared hall). While it is clearly designed to function as a mosque, the building is identified in its foundation inscription not as a mosque but more generically as a 'Dharma-hall' or *dharmasāle* (cf. the Sanskrit *dharmaśālā*), an Indic term traditionally used to designate a charitable rest house where food, water, and lodging are provided. And while built at the behest of a Muslim patron—identified in the inscription as 'the warrior Aḥmad Khān' (*kaṭigeya Āhamuda Khāna*)—the meritorious fruit arising from the foundation (itself an Indic concept) is transferred to Aḥmad Khān's overlord, the reigning 'Hindu' king

Devarāya II.

The building in question is situated in Vijayanagara's so-called Muslim quarter, a once-thriving residential area located along the main northeastern road within the city's urban core. Architecturally, it is a modest pillared hall of fifteen bays, three bays deep and five across (Figure 1). The structure is open across its entire eastern side and enclosed within plain masonry walls on the remaining three sides; it stands on a simple molded base, with access provided by steps in front of the northeastern bay. Centered in the middle bay of the back wall is a rectangular niche, framed by a double-curved arch with a knoblike finial at its top. The hall is flat-roofed, with ceiling slabs laid directly across the beams carried by the columns (Michell 1985: 105–7, 1992: 70, Figures 57, 59, Plate 71).

It is on the side face of one of these ceiling beams—that over the central bay on the building's eastern facade—that the Kannada foundation inscription is incised in five lines. This inscription records the date of the building's dedication and identifies its patron as one Āhamuda Khāna (a Kannada transcription of the Perso-Arabic 'Aḥmad Khān'), a warrior in the service of the reigning king of Vijayanagara, Devarāya II:

> In the year Siddhārthi, on the tenth day of the bright fortnight of the month of Āśvīja [Friday, September 18, 1439], during the reign of Śrīvīrapratāpa Devarāya Mahārāya, the auspicious king of great kings, the supreme ruler, breaker of the pride of enemy kings, establisher of kings who take refuge in him, Lord of the eastern, southern, and western oceans, a threatening hero to kings who err in their ways, a hunter of the elephants who are other kings: The warrior Aḥmad Khān who was in his service made this Dharma-hall and well for the merit of the king. May this foundation be protected for as long as the sun and moon endure! (SII 9/2, no. 447; my translation).

While there is nothing in the wording of the text itself to suggest the building's specific sectarian affiliation, the fact that the building's spatial layout conforms to the liturgical needs of Islamic ritual prayer, taken together with the implications of the structure's immediate architectural surroundings, unquestionably establishes its identity as a mosque. Thus, the building is oriented westward toward the *qiblah*, so that if one stands facing its main inner wall one will be facing in the direction of Mecca. The middle of this *qiblah* wall is interrupted by an arched recess that would have served as a *miḥrāb*, the niche that commemoratively marks the position originally taken by the Prophet Muḥammad when leading prayer. The pillared hall itself is preceded by a raised courtyard provided with several pits lined with pottery rings, which have been interpreted as basins and would thus have held the water (provided from the well also mentioned in

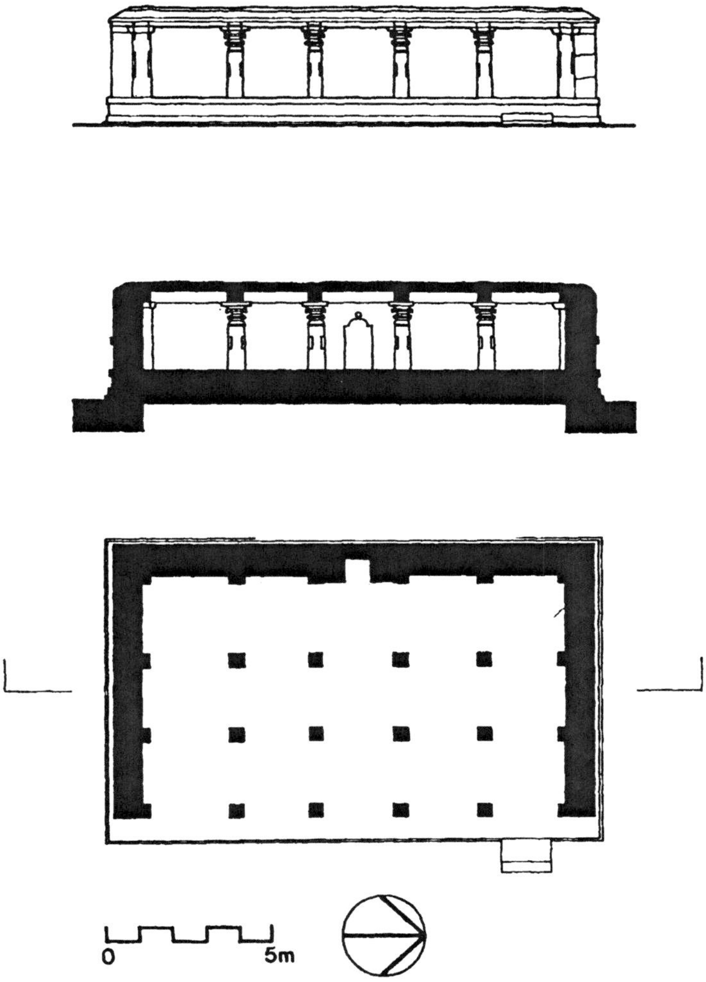

Figure 1. Vijayanagara, Aḥmad Khān's *dharmasāle*, plan, section, and elevation (after Michell 1992).

the foundation inscription) needed for the performance of the ablutions required before ritual prayer. If this is not evidence enough, the Islamic destiny of this 'Dharma-hall' is further underscored by its location within the city's 'Muslim quarter,' a sector of the site that is clearly identifiable both on the basis of contemporary literary testimony and on the basis of its high concentration of Muslim graves and tombs.[8] In fact, one of the more impressive tombs lies just to the south of Aḥmad Khān's mosque and is aligned with it axially.

While the building's identity as a mosque is thus firmly established by its liturgical features and siting, every other feature of the building—from its architectural style to its designation in the inscription as a 'Dharma-hall'—conspires to present it as something else. The building appears not as an exotic edifice devoted to the rites of an alien religion but as a familiar type of religious edifice that can be characterized in terms of *dharma*, the moral principles that are understood within the Indic worldview as the basis of social and cosmic order. Thus, although the building possesses the liturgical features minimally required of a place of prayer, it is not marked, beyond that, with any of the formal signs usually associated with Islamic architecture. It lacks the arches and domes typically found in mosques in more fully Islamicate contexts within the fifteenth-century Deccan, such as at Bijapur or Golconda, but is, instead, built according to the simple trabeate system that had long typified local Indic architectural practice.[9] Indeed, the mosque's columns, with their simply articulated square shafts bearing a series of three superposed capitals, are perfect realizations of a common regional column type known as *citrakhaṇḍa* and are indistinguishable from examples of the type that may be found in the *maṇḍapa* halls of Hindu temples built at Vijayanagara during the same period. Moreover, nowhere in the foundation inscription, apart from the recognizably Perso-Arabic form of the patron's name, is there anything to suggest that this *dharmasāle* served any functions other than those that would have been familiar within the context of an Indic 'rest house.' In fact, so successful was the act of cultural translation that produced this mosque and its associated foundation inscription, that the building's Islamic affiliation does not even appear to have been recognized by modern scholarship until as recently as the 1980s (Michell 1985: 105–7, 1990, 1: 72; Nagaraja Rao 1983: 35, 64–65). Thus, when the inscription was first published in *South Indian inscriptions* in 1941, its findspot was recorded as being 'on [a] mandapa' and its contents were summarized as recording 'the construction of a rest house and a well' (9/2, no. 457)—thus obscuring not only the building's true identity as a mosque but also the very specific ritual sense in which the expression *dharmasāle* was here being employed.

Reflecting upon this evidence, we might naturally ask *why* Aḥmad Khān's mosque was seen as commensurate with an Indic *dharmasāle*, but I would suggest that it is more productive to begin by asking *how* this type of cultural translation was negotiated. Indeed, although the primary sources at our disposal consist of just two pieces of data—the architectural evidence of the building itself, and the textual evidence of the associated foundation inscription—these two pieces of data are so illuminating when taken together, that we may begin to sketch out in some detail a possible answer to this question.

Before proceeding with the substance of this analysis, however, several preliminary observations are in order. In the first place, it is analytically useful, in speaking of Aḥmad Khān's *dharmasāle*, to distinguish between two different sets of actions and their results. On the one hand, there is the primary act of founding the building, which would have comprised varied acts of patronage, planning, design, and construction, resulting ultimately in the realization of the physical edifice itself. On the other hand, there is the secondary act of representing that architectural action as part of a symbolic political transaction, in which the merit accruing from the building's foundation is dedicated to Aḥmad Khān's overlord Devarāya. The tangible product of this act is the epigraphic text inscribed on the edifice. Although these two sets of actions may be distinguished analytically on the basis of differences in purpose (one provides a certain kind of ritual space, while the other serves to articulate and affirm relations of political hierarchy), differences in the human agents involved in implementing them (one calls for a group of artisan-builders, while the other demands an author and an engraver), and differences in the nature of their products (one results in a building, the other in a text), they are at the same time inextricably linked in their historical unfolding. Both acts revolve around the same object, the building; both reflect some of the same cognitive decisions, such as those leading to the representation of a mosque as a *dharmasāle*; and, both are initiated by the same human agent, Aḥmad Khān. Moreover, the two acts are to a certain degree interdependent and mutually condition each other. The act of dedication is of course logically predicated upon the prior completion of the architectural act that produces the building; but we must also recognize the other, less apparent side of this relationship, namely, that the intention of representing this dedicatory act in a certain way—as a record of the transfer of merit—preconditions the act of building itself and effectively constrains some of the choices of planning and design that will be made by the patron and the builders.

Second, we must recognize that whether we are considering the building or the text, the fruit of the act results, in both instances, from a social process of collaboration between the patron (Aḥmad Khān) and a group of productive agents who are instrumental in implementing the patron's intentions. In both cases, Aḥmad Khān must be considered the ultimate instigator of the action, in that it is he who would have initiated the acts of construction and commemoration, established the conditions for their successful realization, and arranged to compensate the respective executive agents for their labor. However, even though we may thus speak loosely of both mosque and inscription as being Aḥmad Khān's, the fact remains that neither would have been possible without the instrumental contribution of these productive agents—the artisan-builders, who would have worked out the details of the design and carried out the actual construction of the building, and the author and engraver, who would have composed the Kannada text of the epigraph and inscribed it onto the one of the structure's stone beams.

As a third point and corollary to the preceding observation, we must also note that the two sets of primary actors in each case—that is, the patron and the productive agents—would each have been bound by different sets of constraints as they proceeded with their respective actions. In building the mosque, Aḥmad Khān would have been constrained by his understanding of the needs of the ultimate beneficiaries of his act—that is, the community of users for whom the mosque was intended—while the artisan-builders would have been bound by the formal concepts, techniques, and methods of the architectural practice in which they had been trained. In the case of the inscription, on the other hand, Aḥmad Khān would have been constrained by his understanding of what was proper and possible in his relationship with Devarāya, the beneficiary of his act of transferring merit, while the author and engraver of the inscription would have been bound by the established formats, formulas, and conceptual language of established Indic epigraphic practice. It is thus clear that each of the two acts we are considering is actually a complex social event, involving in different measure the input of not just two but, in effect, three distinct 'agents,' whether individuals or collective groups. Not only do we have the two primary actors but there is also in each case a third agent who contributes indirectly to the final form taken by the fruit of the act: this is the intended beneficiary of the act (the community of worshippers; the Vijayanagara king) whose perceived interests and needs inform the decisions made by the patron.

How, then, did the collective actions and decisions made by these varied agents serve to negotiate the cultural commensurability of mosque and *dharmasāle*? The first step in the process can be traced, I would suggest, to Aḥmad Khān's decision to construct an edifice that would simultaneously serve two purposes: not just to provide a place of prayer for the local Muslim community but also to bring merit to his overlord, the Vijayanagara king. Had he intended his building to satisfy only the first purpose, it would have been reduced to the less significant status of a neighborhood mosque without any higher-level political functions.[10] It would thus have remained compartmentalized in a separate social space at the margins of public life, obviating any need for exploring its commensurability with local, Indic institutions. Aḥmad Khān, however, did not rest content with founding a simple neighborhood mosque but decided to go further and use the building as a means of affirming his loyalty to Devarāya. The building was thereby thrust squarely within a different and more public social space within the city, thus necessitating the negotiation of a workable set of cultural interpretations. On the one hand, this initial move of Aḥmad Khān's itself constituted the first such act of interpretation, in that it was predicated on his understanding of how the foundation of a mosque might be construed within the terms of local, Indic cultural practice. Specifically, his intention of using the mosque's foundation as a political instrument rested upon the proposition that the act of founding a mosque and its associated well would be analogous to the performance of other charitable acts within an Indic context (such as founding temples, wells, and rest houses). Most importantly, the choice implied that the foundation would produce, in a manner consonant with those acts, religious merit that might be transferred to others. On the other hand, this initial move would also have determined the desirability of employing the formal languages and systems of communication that were locally dominant in order to realize his goals, so as to ensure broad legibility to the king and other members of the court elite who might behold the mosque and inscription. Accordingly, he engaged artisan-builders who worked within an established Indic architectural mode—not in the Islamicate style seen in the adjacent tomb—and an author and engraver who would formulate and inscribe the text of his foundation inscription not in Persian but in the local Kannada language and script.

A second and more concrete step in this process would have been taken in the course of designing and constructing the actual building. Once Aḥmad Khān had engaged a group of builders, his next task would have been to interpret the needs and requirements of the building to them. Given the evidence at hand, it is impossible to know precisely how this information would have been communicated, although several possible scenarios suggest themselves. One would have Aḥmad Khān specifying these requirements in relatively abstract terms, as a series of features or attributes that the building should have in order to satisfy the liturgical needs of ritual prayer. For example, one might imagine him specifying that the building should consist of a covered space preceded by a broad, open area with cisterns for ablutions; that it should have a solid wall on the western side and be open along the east, so as to be oriented toward the *qiblah* of Mecca to the west; and, that there should be an arch-framed niche centered in the western wall to serve as a *miḥrāb*. Alternately, we might imagine Aḥmad Khān communicating these needs in a more concrete fashion, in the form of a description of a given mosque with which he was familiar. If this was the case, we might expect to find him specifying such features even as the number and arrangement of bays within the structure's enclosed space. The likelihood of this latter scenario is underscored by the fact that the particular arrangement of the bays in his *dharmasāle*–mosque is, in fact, a common one in small Deccani mosques, such as that seen in the *dargāh* of Mujarrad Kāmāl at Gulbarga, which was most likely built in the last quarter of the fourteenth century or in the opening decades of the fifteenth (Merklinger 1981: catalogue 18, plan 3).[11] However we imagine Aḥmad Khān communicating his needs and intentions, it is clear that the local builders' comprehension of those requirements would have been mediated through a series of cognitive filters provided by the conceptual categories upon which Indic architectural practice was based. In specific terms, one suspects that they would have recognized in Aḥmad Khān's description a close match with the indigenous building type known as the *maṇḍapa*, a flat-roofed, pillared hall generally of a single story, that may be either open at the sides or enclosed within solid walls. More particularly, if Aḥmad Khān had expressed his needs in terms of a description of a mosque like that in the *dargāh* of Mujarrad Kāmāl, it would have called to mind a specific type of *maṇḍapa* that was defined both in South Indian prescriptive architectural treatises and in local practice at Vijayanagara. The *Mayamata*, for example, recognizes two major classes of *maṇḍapa*, those that are square in plan and those based on a rectangle; within the rectangular category, one type of plan is distinguished—the so-called *dhanamaṇḍapa*—which consists of fifteen bays arranged in a three-by-five pattern (25.115b–16). Whether the *Mayamata* was actually known at Vijayanagara, a *maṇḍapa* plan corresponding to its *dhana*-type is in fact represented at the site in a two-storied variant found at the end of the chariot street in the Virūpākṣa temple. Significantly, this *maṇḍapa* also happens to be enclosed within solid walls along its two short ends and one long side, the other long side remaining open. Having thus understood Aḥmad Khān's architectural needs in terms of familiar Indic building typology, the builders would have proceeded to execute his commission by constructing a *maṇḍapa*-like structure for him. Wherever he had called for specific formal features to satisfy the building's liturgical requirements—as in the case of the *miḥrāb* niche in the middle of the back wall—the builders were careful to provide those details. But wherever he had passed over structural or formal details in his description of the model mosque—as he evidently must have done by omitting reference to the particular structural system of piers, arches, and domes making up each bay in a building like the Mujarrad Kāmāl mosque—the local builders simply would have followed the dictates of local tradition and provided the structures and forms that would have been employed in building an ordinary *maṇḍapa*: the usual *citrakhaṇḍa* columns, beams, and flat-ceiling slabs.

A final aspect of the hermeneutic process may be identified in the series of cognitive operations that would have led the author of the epigraphic text to recognize Aḥmad Khān's mosque as a *dharmasāle*. Here two distinct possibilities suggest themselves, differing in accordance with the degree of specificity that we choose to read into the inscription's term '*dharmasāle.*' On the one hand, this term may be taken in the very general sense of a 'hall of *dharma,*' that is, as a building devoted to *dharma* or the observance of religious practices. If this was the sense in which the term was intended, then the author's choice of this expression would have rested upon a general perception that the building was destined to serve as a religious edifice for Aḥmad Khān and his coreligionists, much as a temple would function as the site of religious practices for local worshippers of gods such as Śiva and Viṣṇu. In such a usage, the term '*dharmasāle*' would thus compare closely with the formulation *dharmasthāna* ('site of religion') that is used in the well-known Sanskrit inscription from Verāval in Gujarat (C.E. 1264) in referring to a mosque (also called by a transliterated form of '*masjid,*' *mijigiti*) founded by one Noradina Piroja (Nūr al-Dīn Fīrūz), a ship's captain originally from Hormuz (EI 34: 141–50; Chattopadhyaya 1998: 71–78).

On the other hand, if we consider the overall wording of Aḥmad Khān's inscription and relate it to local patterns of patronage and epigraphic practice within the immediate region of the Deccan, it appears likely that the term '*dharmasāle*' would have been intended in a far more specific sense. In the first place, within the text of Aḥmad Khān's inscription itself, the word '*dharma*' is used two further times in different but closely related senses, which help delimit the possible range of meanings carried by the term in the compound *dharmasāle.* Thus, in the expression I have rendered as 'for the merit of the king' (*rāyarige dharmavāga bēkemdu*), the term '*dharma*' is used in the specific sense of 'merit,' a well-established epigraphic usage in both Kannada and Telugu. The term is used yet again in the expression I have translated as 'may this foundation be protected' (*yī dharmmavanu pālisudu*), this time in the sense of the object that is founded for the production of merit, that is, the *dharmasāle.* Given this immediate context, I believe we may safely conclude that the author of the inscription did not have the generic meaning of 'religious edifice' in mind when he called the mosque a *dharmasāle* but was seeing the building as a 'hall' that would generate religious merit through its foundation, by virtue of the fact that it was a public charitable institution destined to serve the good of others and not just the immediate interests of the patron.

Such an interpretation is additionally in accordance with the patterns of terminology used in this region to refer to a variety of charitable foundations that were understood to function in this way. Thus there are medieval epigraphs recording the foundation or endowment of charitable water troughs for animals (Telugu *dharmagāḍi*); charitable water tanks for public use (Telugu *dharmakōnēru*); and, what is of particular significance in the present context, charitable rest houses or feeding houses for pilgrims, wayfarers, or the indigent

(Telugu *dharmasatramu*) (for epigraphic references, see Dutt 1967: 152–53; Suryakumari 1982: 84–85). This last type of establishment is also known in both Telugu and Kannada as *satraśāla/satraśāle* or *dharmaśāla/dharmaśāle*, which thus suggests that the author of Aḥmad Khān's inscription would have had in mind not just a charitable hall of uncertain purpose but specifically one where water, food, and accommodations would have been provided to those in need. Such a perception might have been based, in part, on an accurate understanding of some of the charitable functions that would actually have been served by Aḥmad Khān's mosque; but I suspect that it would equally well have been conditioned by the patron's perception of the similarity between the mosque and the *dharmasāle* as architectural types. While an architectural history of the *dharmaśāla* remains to be written and there is accordingly little information available as to the precise forms that these institutions took, the evidence does suggest that they would most often have taken the form of *maṇḍapa*s. Thus, according to Pushpa Prasad (1990: 7n17), the term '*sattramaṇḍapa*' is used in Sanskrit texts as a synonym of *sattraśālā* or *dharmaśālā*, thereby implying the generic form of a flat-roofed, pillared hall; and, of more immediate relevance, there is at least one architecturally identifiable *sattraśālā* at the Vijayanagara site which does indeed take the form of a simple, pillared *maṇḍapa*—in this case, a single row of three bays that is open on the sides.[12]

What, then, does the case of Aḥmad Khān's *dharmasāle* contribute to our understanding of the hermeneutics of cultural interpretation? Perhaps most importantly, it demonstrates in the most vivid manner just how socially embedded and historically contingent the process is. The conclusion that a mosque is equivalent to a *dharmasāle* is not one that is made merely at the level of abstract discursive thought, whether that be imagined in the form of an individual's reflective contemplation or of a quiet conversation between individuals interested in locating shared values and practices. Rather, it is a conclusion that must be socially negotiated by many different actors, representing distinct social, economic, political, and cultural interests, as they all collaborate in a common series of linked and mutually conditioning actions. Just as importantly, the case suggests just how much the process depends upon the discovery of fortuitous areas of convergence between the two cultures in question. Thus, the fact that both Indic and Islamicate traditions of architectural practice within the region knew of enclosed, rectangular halls of three-by-five bays, with an open, pillared facade across one of the long sides, was a factor of considerable importance in determining the specific course of the hermeneutic operation. This fortuitous area of convergence not only made it easier for the builders to comprehend and satisfy Aḥmad Khān's spatial needs but, in turn, their decision to capitalize upon this fortuitous similarity also contributed to the perception that the building thus produced could meaningfully be understood as a *dharmasāle* as well as a mosque. Again, we have a crucial element of ambiguity—an ambiguity not only of architectural form but also of social function—that is essential in that it enables cultural meanings to be generated that move simultaneously in two different directions.[13] Neither set of meanings exhausts the building's semiotic potential, and therein lies its significance to the hermeneutics of cultural interpretation. If we arbitrarily decide to call it either a mosque or a *dharmasāle* alone, then we have fallen unwittingly into the intellectual straightjacket of communalism and failed to achieve our goal of a historical understanding of the past.

The cases of ʿAin al-Mulk Gīlāni and Aḥmad Khān are admittedly just two examples, but they suggest in the clearest possible terms the perils of imposing contemporary communal categories upon the premodern past. Attempts to comprehend the medieval history of the Deccan in terms of Hindu and Muslim opposition are bound to miss the mark, not because they predispose us to misrepresent the nature of the Hindu-Muslim encounter as one of conflict but, more fundamentally, because the very terms of analysis themselves are misconceived. The problem is not simply that Hindus and Muslims did not always relate through violence, conflict, and opposition but rather that the categories 'Hindu' and 'Muslim' had not yet emerged as primary bases of identity in this medieval society. This is not to ignore the existence of significant cultural differences between Indic and Islamicate modes of organizing human experience nor to deny the presence of what Talbot (1995: 694) has termed 'incipient cores of ethnicity' in the medieval period, which would eventually transform into the familiar categories of communal identity. But what is clear, from our consideration of the careers and actions of ʿAin al-Mulk Gīlāni and Aḥmad Khān, is that at the elite level, at least, class-based forms of identity were ultimately more fundamental than those based on religious practices and that these identities served to unite individuals who might otherwise differ in terms of religious affiliation. And, moreover, as would naturally be expected given the regular movements and interactions of these individuals, we may conclude that the very boundaries between Indic and Islamicate culture were highly permeable and that they shifted and yielded constantly as efforts were made to find underlying areas of similarity and congruence.

Notes

1. This chapter is based in part on papers presented at the Forty-Sixth Annual Meeting of the Association for Asian Studies (Boston, 1994) and the Twenty-Fifth Annual Wisconsin Conference on South Asia (Madison, 1996). I am deeply indebted to my fellow panelists on both occasions, Cynthia Talbot and

Richard Eaton, for their invaluable collaboration and inspiration over the years. I am further beholden to Richard Eaton for advice and information, which has helped me find my way across the 'Maginot line' of Indian historiography, and to William Pinch for his suggestion of an inspired title, which has enabled me—once again—to clarify my thinking on important matters of substance.

2. We should note here that several different individuals appear in the pages of Firishta with the title 'Ain al-Mulk (literally, 'essence of the kingdom') and that the individual being considered here—'Ain al-Mulk Gīlāni ('Ein-ool-Moolk Geelany,' in Briggs' transcription)—must be carefully distinguished from these other 'Ain al-Mulks. These other figures include:

(1) Saif Khān 'Ain al-Mulk ('Seif Khan Ein-ool-Moolk'), who serves Golconda under Jamshīd Qūlī Quṭb Shāh but is then exiled to Ahmadnagar by Jamshīd; is called back by the dowager upon Subḥān Qūlī Quṭb Shāh's accession; assumes too much power and is forced to flee in the month of Rajab in the year 1550 CE (Firishta 1966, 3: 232, 234–36);

(2) Saif al-Dīn 'Ain al-Mulk ('Seif-ood-Deen Ein-ool-Moolk'), who serves Ahmadnagar under Burhān Niẓām Shāh and leads an attack on Ibrāhīm 'Ādil Shāh I's camp during the month of Ramaḍān (1550); takes refuge at Berar upon the accession of Ḥusayn Shāh (1554); takes up service, one year later, at Bijapur under Ibrāhīm 'Ādil Shāh I and becomes alienated from Ibrāhīm in about 1556 due to a misunderstanding during a battle over Sholapur with the Ahmadnagar forces. He attempts to carve out his own principality, attacks Bijapur, and is forced to flee, taking refuge at Ahmadnagar, where he is assassinated (Firishta 1966, 3: 63–68, 145);

(3) 'Ain al-Mulk ('Ein-ool-Moolk'), a title given to one Qābūl Khān ('Kubool Khan'), who serves Ibrāhīm Quṭb Shāh (Firishta 1966, 3: 238–39); and,

(4) 'Ain al-Mulk ('Ein-ool-Moolk'), an officer of Bijapur who is not characterized otherwise, marches toward Ahmadnagar with Aṃkuśa Khān ('Ankoos Khan') for purpose of plunder and is killed (1567; Firishta 1966, 3: 81).

3. Another inscription, dated 1562, identifies the territory of Dummesima as his *amaraṃ* estate (EC 7: Ci. 69).

4. And on, one might argue, through the person of the emperor all the way up to Virūpākṣa, the state deity who was held to be the owner of state land within the kingdom and whose 'signature' closes the grant and, thus, testifies to the validity of the transaction (for the significance of this epigraphic practice, see Verghese 1995: 19, 141–54).

5. It should be noted that Marathi, the Indo-European language that was dominant in the northern districts of the Bijapur territory, was also widely used as an administrative language by the Bijapur state.

6. One imagines, however, that these loan words might just as well have

entered Dakhni via Marathi, which was widely used as an administrative language in the Bijapur kingdom. Another possibility, suggested by Carla Petievich (personal communication, 1999), is that the Sanskritic element in Dakhni might have entered directly from Sanskrit, rather than being mediated through an Indic vernacular, whether Dravidian or Indo-European. Clearly, there is a pressing need for more research on the linguistic history of medieval Dakhni, with particular reference to its relations with other languages used contemporaneously in the Deccan.

7. Clearly, the cultural code switching represented by 'Ain al-Mulk's *agrahāram* grant worked in both directions. An intriguing counterpart to 'Ain al-Mulk is offered by the case of the Marāṭhā chief Mālojī, who, as a 'Hindu' servant of the Islamicate Niẓām Shāhī court, named his sons after a Ṣūfī *pīr* and was buried in an Islamicate type tomb (see the discussion in James Laine, in this volume).

8. Domingo Paes, who was at Vijayanagara between 1520 and 1522, mentions the city's 'Moorish quarter' in the course of his description of a road which leads from the 'great open space' (*terreira*) that is 'in the middle of the city' (this plaza is archaeologically identifiable as 'Enclosure I'; see Fritz, Michell, and Nagaraja Rao 1984: Figure 3.2) and runs to the 'other side of the city,' that is, the northeast, since Paes's description is based on an approach to the city from Nagalapuram (= Hospet) that lies to the southwest (Sewell 1962: 246). This road is thus identifiable with the city's main northeast artery ('NE'; see Fritz, Michell, and Nagaraja Rao 1984: Figure 2.4). Paes goes on to describe this street in great detail, noting the many houses of merchants and the evening markets in the segment before the gate in the inner wall, the houses and shops of craftsmen in the segment beyond in the urban core, and, finally, the 'Moorish quarter at the end of this street,' 'at the very end of the city' (Sewell 1962: 247), all of which fits perfectly with the features documented archaeologically and epigraphically along the city's great 'northeastern' road (see Michell 1985).

9. It should be noted that trabeate mosques were in fact built in the Deccan but appear to be limited to those cases in which older, pre-existing Indic columns were being appropriated as spolia and where their use served the process Grabar has termed the 'symbolic appropriation of the land' (1987: 43). In the Deccan, as in the core territory of the Delhi Sulṭānate, the construction of such mosques appears to have been concentrated in the early phases of the extension of Islamic rule into the region; thus the trabeate construction and columns used as spolia in the Quwwāt al-Islām Masjid in Delhi (1193–1311) and the Aṛhāī Dīn kā Jhoṁpṛā Masjid in Ajmer (c. 1205) yield in the fourteenth century to the arcuate, rubble, and mortar construction of monuments such as Delhi's Begampurī (c. 1343) and Khiṛkī (c. 1352–54) *masjids* (see Hoag 1977: 282–88; Welch and Crane 1983: 130–40). Similarly, some of the earliest Deccani mosques, such as that of Karīm

al-Dīn at Bijapur (1320), founded just two years after Delhi's annexation of the region, use Indic columns as spolia (Eaton 1978: 15–17); but by the end of the fourteenth century, construction based on domes, arches, and masonry piers was nearly universal, and spolia were rarely used (Merklinger 1981). One significant exception is provided by an important group of sixteenth-century mosques from Raichur and its environs, which continue to use spolia and trabeate construction (Merklinger 1981: catalogues 68, 70, 76, 112). This usage would appear to be related to the status of the Raichur Doāb as a contested territory that passed repeatedly back and forth between Bijapur and Vijayanagara.

10. The important political functions usually attributed to mosques in fact belong properly only to the *Masjid al-jāmi'* (congregational mosque), whence the collective Friday noon prayer is performed and the *khuṭbah* delivered in the name of the caliph by his governor or representative. Ideally, there is only one such congregational mosque in each city (or constituent ward in very large urban centers). In contrast to the *Masjid al-jāmi'* is the ordinary *masjid*, of which considerable numbers might be built in any larger village, town, or city, typically in the form of small, unpretentious buildings, to provide a center of activity for a neighborhood, tribal, or sectarian group. Although such buildings clearly fulfilled important social functions, they would in most cases have had little significance in the context of the broader political order (Pederson 1991: 331–32, 335–37).

11. The three-by-five bay plan type is in fact traceable back to Tughluq Delhi, where it occurs in the sanctuary of the two-story Kalān Masjid, built in 1387 (Welch and Crane 1983: 133, Figure 4). Although dating from a later period, examples at Raichur (the Ek mīnār kī Masjid, dated 1513) and Bijapur (the mosque in the Ibrāhīm Rawẓa complex, c. 1626) attest to the continuing importance of the type in the Deccan (Merklinger 1981: plans 15, 27).

12. This building is referred to in an inscription dated 1199 CE, which records a series of religious donations made to the various gods and institutions at the site by one Maiduna Cauḍayya (SII 4, no. 260). Of relevance here is the endowment made by Cauḍayya 'to enable the offering of hospitality and the serving of meals for ten Brāhmaṇas in the alms house (*satrasāle*) to the right of Virūpākṣadēva' (SII 4, no. 260, lines 78–79; my translation). This *satrasāle* may still be recognized today, in the archaic, three-bayed *maṇḍapa* structure that is preserved just to the south of the Virūpākṣa shrine (i.e., to the right of the god since he faces east), now largely obscured within the larger pillared hall that has engulfed it on every side (Wagoner 1996: 162).

13. This calls to mind Stewart Gordon's discussion (in this volume) of Per Otnes' emphasis on the 'mediator'—'generally an artifact which both self and other, to some degree, "share" ' (p.228)—as a key element in the analysis of identity and the historically contingent relationships between self and other.

References Cited

Chattopadhyaya, Brajadulal. 1998. *Representing the Other? Sanskrit Sources and the Muslims (Eighth to Fourteenth Century)*. Delhi: Manohar.

Dutt, Kunduri Iswara. 1967. *Inscriptional Glossary of Andhra Pradesh*. Hyderabad: Andhra Pradesh Sahitya Akademi.

Eaton, Richard M. 1978. *Sufis of Bijapur, 1300–1700: Social Roles of Sufis in Medieval India*. Princeton: Princeton University Press.

EC. 1889–1955. *Epigraphia Carnatica*. 16 vols. Bangalore: Government Press.

EI. 1892–1978. *Epigraphia Indica*. 42 vols. New Delhi: Archaeological Survey of India.

Firishta, Muḥammad Abū al-Qāsim. 1966 [1829]. *History of the Rise of the Mahomedan Power in India Till the Year AD 1612, Translated from the Original Persian of Mahomed Kasim Ferishta* (trans. John Briggs). 4 vols. Calcutta: Editions Indian.

Fritz, John M., George Michell, and M. S. Nagaraja Rao. 1984. *Where Kings and Gods Meet: The Royal Centre at Vijayanagara, India*. Tucson: University of Arizona Press.

Grabar, Oleg. 1987 [1973]. *The Formation of Islamic Art*. New Haven, CT: Yale University Press.

Hayavadana Rao, C. 1930. *Mysore Gazetteer, Compiled for Government*. Volume 2: *Historical*. Part 3: *Medieval: From the Foundation of the Vijayanagara Kingdom to the Destruction of Vijayanagara by Tipū Sultān in 1776*. Bangalore: Government Press.

Hoag, John D. 1977. *Islamic Architecture*. New York: Abrams.

Mayamata. 1970–76. *Mayamata: Traité Sanskrit d'architecture* (ed. and trans. Bruno Dagens). 2 vols. Pondicherry: Institut Français d'Indologie.

Merklinger, Elizabeth Schotten. 1981. *Indian Islamic Architecture: The Deccan, 1347–1686*. Warminster: Aris and Phillips.

Michell, George. 1985. "Architecture of the Muslim Quarters at Vijayanagara." *In* M. S. Nagaraja Rao, ed., *Vijayanagara: Progress of Research, 1983–84*, 101–18. Mysore: Directorate of Archaeology and Museums.

Michell, George. 1990. *Vijayanagara: Architectural Inventory of the Urban Core*. 2 vols. Mysore: Directorate of Archaeology and Museums.

Michell, George. 1992. *The Vijayanagara Courtly Style: Incorporation and Synthesis in the Royal Architecture of Southern India, 15th–17th Centuries*. New Delhi: Manohar.

Nagaraja Rao, M. S., ed. 1983. *Vijayanagara: Progress of Research, 1979–83*. Mysore: Directorate of Archaeology and Museums.

Pederson, J. 1991 [1953]. "Masdjid." *In* H. A. R. Gibb and J. H. Kramers, eds., *Shorter Encyclopaedia of Islam*, 330–53. Leiden: E. J. Brill.

Prasad, Pushpa. 1990. *Sanskrit Inscriptions of Delhi Sultanate, 1191–1526.* Delhi: Oxford University Press.

Sewell, Robert. 1962 [1900]. *A Forgotten Empire (Vijayanagara): A Contribution to the History of India.* Delhi: Government of India.

SII. 1890–1940. *South Indian Inscriptions.* 20 vols. Madras: Government Press.

Sircar, D. C. 1965. *Indian Epigraphy.* Delhi: Motilal Banarsidass.

Suryakumari, A. 1982. *The Temple in Āndhradeśa.* Madurai: Sarvodaya Ilakkiya Pannai.

Svarājyalakṣmī, V. 1979. Telugulō Anyadēśyālu. *In* Bh. Krishnamurti, ed., *Telugu Bhāṣācaritra,* 326–42. Hyderābād: Āndhra Pradeśa Sāhitya Akādemī.

Talbot, Cynthia M. 1995. "Inscribing the Other, Inscribing the Self: Hindu-Muslim Identities in Pre-colonial India." *Comparative Studies in Society and History* 37, 4: 692–722.

Verghese, Anila. 1995. *Religious Traditions at Vijayanagara: As Revealed Through the Monuments.* Delhi: Manohar.

Wagoner, Phillip B. 1993. *Tidings of the King: A Translation and Ethnohistorical Analysis of the Rāyavācakamu.* Honolulu: University of Hawaii Press.

Wagoner, Phillip B. 1996. "From 'Paṁpā's Crossing' to 'the Place of Lord Virupāksha': Architecture, Cult, and Patronage at Hampi before the Founding of Vijayanagara." *In* D. V. Devaraj and Channabasappa S. Patil, eds., *Vijayanagara: Progress of Research 1988–91,* 141–74. Mysore: Directorate of Archaeology and Museums.

Welch, Anthony, and Howard Crane. 1983. The Tughluqs: Master Builders of the Delhi Sultanate. *Muqarnas: An Annual on Islamic Art and Architecture* 1: 123–66.

Surprising Bedfellows: Vaiṣṇava and Shīʿa Alliance in Kavi Āriph's 'Tale of Lālmon'

Tony K. Stewart

THE LITERATURES OF SATYA PĪR

The literature of the so-called Hindu-Muslim holy figure of Satya Pīr has eluded analysis because it presents an image of religiosity that seems to violate contemporary sensibilities regarding what is supposedly proper for the religions' constituents. It is precisely this problematic aspect that makes Satya Pīr a potentially important window into the processes by which these two dominant Bengali religious traditions encountered one another historically, and specifically how each envisioned the other, for the mere existence of these tales and the very image of Satya Pīr himself suggest that this encounter was not always produced in a contentious or alienating environment. The cultic dimension of Satya Pīr's worship has always been, by its own admission, ritually thin—its greatest elaborations taking place in the household ritual (*vrata* vow) cycle of Hindu women, and there in an extremely truncated form compared to other deities so honored; elsewhere the aniconic ritual is an offering of a simple concoction of rice flour, banana, milk, and spices called *śirṇī*. Not surprisingly, there have been no institutional structures apart from the recitation of his tales and the limited offerings made to procure his aid in creating wealth and general weal. What Satya Pīr has had, and continues to have, are stories, lots of stories, a narrative literature that is arguably the second largest premodern literature in the Bengali language.[1]

Devoid of overt theology beyond the palest expressions of an often vague connection to divinity, and an equally limited ritual structure devoid of even the semblance of social institutions, there seems to be very little demonstrable connection of Satya Pīr to the actual lives of Bengalis. Yet his stories have proliferated for more than four centuries, and his name is instantly recognized even today. The narratives of his adventures, and of those who worship him, speak to the imagination. In this they provide a possibly crucial insight into this frontier region, a place where the tried and true rules of more settled lands do not seem to have adhered, where improvisation and contingency have always been a part of daily living, where all manner of men and women have come into contact, making up the rules as they negotiated these unpredictable encounters. These tales speak to the search for survival among peoples who must rely on their own devices, away from the time-honored institutions found in more settled lands, pointing vividly to the impossible task penury places on people who try to be moral. This commentary was true in the sixteenth and seventeenth centuries when the frontier brought together Hindus and Muslims in a largely rural Bengal, and it has adapted itself into the growing metropolitan centers of the colonial and now postcolonial period as well. It is a literature that speculates and entertains, exaggerating to discover what might be, as much as what has to be in the pragmatic terms necessary for comprehending the often surreal experience of life. Beyond the occasional statement that equates Nārāyaṇa-Viṣṇu and Allāh and the enjoinders to worship, there is no overt religious content. What is there is vague and ill defined and, in the nature of fiction everywhere, only indirectly points to its ideological experiments. It is through action of the narrative itself that this experimentation can be detected.

For our purposes, these narratives—the earliest of which date to the late sixteenth century—can be grouped into three broad thematic categories. The first two are relatively straightforward; it is the third category of the romance on which we will focus because the texts do not yield any readily religious explanation as the others do, even though they are part of Satya Pīr's cycle. The first and most widespread—although it is not altogether clear if this is historically the earliest strain—is a literature that is overtly Vaiṣṇava, seeing in Satya Pīr an *avatāra* (descent) of Lord Viṣṇu. In the consistently structured sequence of these Vaiṣṇava tales, Satya Pīr (who is also routinely called by the name 'Satya Nārāyaṇa') first aids an old Brāhmaṇa who has been reduced to penury. He does this only after arguing to that faithful Brāhmaṇa that the differences between Muslims and Hindus are limited to appearances, to surface images, a position he subsequently 'proves' by manifesting his six-armed form from amidst his Pīr's tattered garments. Overwhelmed by the spectacle, the Brāhmaṇa immediately proffers the requested *śirṇī* and is just as quickly made wealthy. As instructed, he shares this news with any who will listen. A group of woodcutters, frontiersmen of the hardiest sort, observed the sudden change in the Brāhmaṇa, and when they inquire he explains how it happened. They do as instructed and reap the rewards, building massive forts and embattlements along with their dwellings. Later, too, an adventurous merchant benefits in much the same way in his journeys to the edges of the earth (usually South India). These three tales—the poor Brāhmaṇa, the woodcutters, and the merchant—each in innumerable permutations constitute the core of the Vaiṣṇava literary tradition.[2] The second major group is composed of tales that are overtly Islamic in orientation, where Satya Pīr is an itinerant holy man (albeit somewhat eclectic in his garb) who uses freely Sanskrit, Arabic, and Persian texts. He reveals a propensity to employ magic to make his point, but in tireless effort—and against considerable odds—he instructs the populace from king to *qāẓī* to cowherd in the dangers of self-aggrandizement and hubris, not to mention the ill treatment of mendicants and the general abuse of religion in all its forms.[3] In these two broad groups of tales can be observed distinct tendencies for one tradition to appropriate parts of the other into its own cosmological structures (especially prominent on the Vaiṣṇava side) as well as arguments for mutual recognition and accommodation (especially evident on the Islamic side).[4] It is, however, the third strain of this literature that presents the most difficulties for interpretation—and the one to which we now turn—because its narratives appear not to be in any way overtly religious. Because of their general thematic orientation and construction of plot, we will simply refer to these tales as 'romances.' The action is inevitably impelled by the shadowy figure of Satya Pīr, but Satya Pīr himself remains just offstage and overt religious speculation is glaringly absent.

THE ROMANCES OF SATYA PĪR

The romances of Satya Pīr are elaborate tales of adventure, and in this they share much with the popular *maṅgala kāvya* genre of middle period Bengali literature, semi-epic tales that extol the virtues of one of the popular goddesses (such as Caṇḍī, Manasā, Śītalā) or even the occasional gods (Dharma Ṭhākura) and godlings (the lord of tigers Dakṣiṇa Rāya). In length and twist of plot, they also demonstrate features common to the shorter publicly performed *pāla*, *gāna*, *pāñcālī*, and *kecchā* (Urdu *qissā*) repertory, many of which are designed for highly entertaining public performances. In the star-crossed predicaments of their heroes and heroines, many of whose confusions result from untimely or ill-advised romantic liaisons, their lives are always complicated by a crucial failure to worship Satya Pīr as promised. They share many common tropes to suggest a strong affinity with Bengali versions of the extensive formal romance literature that developed in Avadhi and Hindi as well, stories, such as *Candāyana*, *Padmāvata*, and *Madhumālatī*, which lend themselves to allegorical interpretation.[5] In short, Satya Pīr's romances seem to occupy a somewhat fluid middle ground between other well-established genres without conforming precisely to any, suggesting a connection between their malleable forms and their creative plots; they are innovative, if not genuinely experimental, in nature.

The source of this innovation in the narratives themselves is often the resourcefulness of female protagonists, women who are thrust into unusual (often life and certainly honor threatening) situations, usually as the result of ill-considered decisions and hasty or arrogant acts of their fathers, lovers, or husbands, and who are subsequently saved by husbands, sons, and nephews. As the characters are swept along in concatenations of dismal prospects, each decision and seeming resolution leading to further compromises and dangers. These women, and often their lovers or other young male leads, must makeup their path as they pursue it, trying desperately to impose or extract order where there appears to be none. This situation creativity is of course not at all unlike that of many traditional tales; it is not just that they undergo these moments of crisis, but it is the way they respond that leads to dramatic personal transformations, revealing the host of possibilities open to the main characters, many of which could not be ordinarily sanctioned in the ideals of a traditional society. These characters choose unconventional paths in order to gain or regain conventional ends that would be otherwise out of grasp, certainly to those who failed to put their faith in Satya Pīr. It is this improvisation that reveals a willingness on the part of the authors to explore novel interactions that challenge and confirm what is proper conduct in this world, moving away from the predictable and stable world of predictable moral choices into a realm in which individuals are faced with unheard of problems that require completely novel responses. These stories go far beyond the mechanized application of the religiously or socially prescriptive, which would simply pass on and reaffirm set responses to set situations; they move into a realm of shifting contingencies in which the innovative responses of the protagonists uncover the very logic of their value—and ideological—positions.

Gayārāma's *Madanamañjarī pāla* (1926),[6] a tale that demonstrates a young woman's dedication to her husband, tells the story of a princess who, because of a rash promise by her father the king, is given in marriage to a six-month-old son of a minister named Candrasena. Rather than submit to such humiliation, she flees the bridal chamber with her baby husband, finally settling into a neighboring kingdom, where—with the occasional and timely aid of Satya Pīr—she raises the child. This reversal is structurally opposed to the emergence of the *kulīn* marriage norm within Bengali society, a situation in which old Brāhmaṇa men would marry numerous child brides in order to save the caste ranking of the bride's family but who were subsequently abandoned to their father's family after the collection of dowries (Chakraborty 1963; for some of the background conditions that led to this practice, see Inden 1976). In this opposite case—opposite not only because of the age reversal but also in the actions of the bride who remains dedicated to her husband despite the arrangement—the boy is raised and educated by his wife who has doubled as his mother. With the help of his teacher, the young pubescent man eventually 'uncovers' his true relationship to his 'mother-wife.'[7] Once confirmed, they fall in love, consummate their marriage, and seem to live happily for a while in an idyllic world (no comment is made regarding the local response to this sudden change of their family status). The idyll cannot last; one day on his way to the *bāẓār*, Candrasena is bewitched by a voluptuous *mālinī* (garland weaver) who with the aid of a magic garland transforms him into a tropical parakeet. Parakeet by day, he is made her love slave by night. But a local wealthy patron of the *mālinī*, a princess named Hemalatā, covets and then takes the parakeet only to discover that her own *pūjā* to Lord Śiva for a husband has suddenly, and in ways unexpected, paid dividends. She tells no one, and for months they make passionate love until the inevitable. When she can no longer hide her pregnancy, the king and queen discover the ruse, but the king, being practical, wants no scandal. He arranges to marry his daughter to Candrasena. When the news finally breaks, the first wife Madanamañjarī is fetched and grants her permission for this strange liaison. Shortly after Candrasena returns with his two wives to the kingdom of their origin, meeting his and Madanamañjarī's parents in joyful reunion and the perpetual worship of Satya Pīr.

Many of these same ideals of fidelity and submission (*satī*) are echoed in Kiṅkara's (1923) story of the faithfulness of Rambhāvatī, the wife of a prominent merchant. To allay the merchant's fears that she will be seduced in his long absence, Rambhāvatī gives him a magic garland that promises to stay fresh as long as she is faithful. Mollified, and with a promise to maintain an offering to Satya Pīr, he departs, but the intrigue of the garland invites test after test. Because she is faithful he is successful, but in his eagerness to return to his fabled mate, he forgets Satya Pīr, who wrecks his ships. With his tiger mount salivating over the neck of the prostrate merchant, Satya Pīr extracts a renewed promise, restores the merchant's wealth, and sends him home to his ever faithful wife. The merchant's fortunes are clearly hinged on the action of his wife, and the message to women (especially evident when the narrative is reduced in this truncated form) could hardly be clearer. The impossibility of a garland staying fresh for so long likewise serves as an ambiguous social commentary.

While men in these tales often venture forth to vindicate wrongs done to their women, just as often women hold in their actions the fates of their husbands and sons. In Kiṅkara's *Matilālera pāla* (1914a), Satya Pīr abandons his abode in Mecca in order to find a person worthy of propagating his worship; both men and women are put to the test. A merchant from Rāṅgapura is chosen, although Satya Pīr is compelled to assume the form of Śiva, the merchant's favorite deity, in order to be received by him on his journey. Discovering through a dream that a son conceived at a particularly auspicious moment would spit pearls when he cooed in his mother's arms, Satya Pīr complies with the eager merchant's wish and in the wink of an eye spirits him the hundreds of miles back to his wife, Śīlāvatī. At first disbelieving, she reluctantly succumbs to the advances of her midnight visitor, but when she awakes from this conjugal slumber, she discovers that he has been spirited away as easily as he arrived. With the evidence of her infidelity abounding, the merchant's wife was cast out and branded a harlot by her ever vigilant mother-in-law. A compassionate *wazīr* took pity on the young woman and intervened, but Śīlāvatī was again cast out as soon as she came to term, this time by the jealous wife of the *wazīr*. A wandering *yogī* divined the truth of her plight, and reckoning her to be a modern-day Sītā, he and his wife opened their home to her. The child was born, but the *wazīr*'s wife had at the same time delivered her own stillborn boy; because of her festering agitation over her husband's ministrations to the pregnant Śīlāvatī, the *wazīr*'s wife arranged for the midwife to switch the babies at the home of the *yogī*. Inconsolable at her misfortune, Śīlāvatī abandoned her substitute child to the funeral pyre and wandered aimlessly, no point left to her existence. But a compassionate flower vendor and weaver of garlands took pity and persuaded her to join her humble abode. Eventually through a tortured series of chance happenings—made possible by Satya Pīr's timely intervention—Śīlāvatī discovered that her own son lived. She promptly divined the cause of her misfortune, then publicly accused the *wazīr* of theft. She proved it in court by claiming that the child would spit pearls when he called her 'mother.' Before the understandably skeptical court, she was proved right. The king, who had been especially severe because of the perceived frivolity of her proof, rewarded the young boy, Matilāla, with his own daughter's hand as compensation for the ill treatment of Śīlāvatī and bestowed on him a kingdom. The boy's first official act was to launch a search for his lost father. When his father was found—and not without a certain amount of chiding for having compromised the boy's mother that fateful night—the family was reunited and instituted the worship of Satya Pīr. The morality of this and tales like it, while somewhat obscure with respect to the treatment of single mothers, generally rewards ethically superior behavior by both sexes with pecuniary restoration or even gain and overall elevation in social hierarchies. True to the name of their guardian figure, it is 'truth' that seems to be rewarded by Satya Pīr, truth tempered by devotion to him.

A number of the stories grow significantly more convoluted, spreading the complicity for questionable acts among siblings and even multiple generations; both the problems and their solutions set in motion by one figure can only be resolved as entire families are swallowed into the labyrinth of moral intrigue. Dvīja Kavibara's *Bāghāmbarera pāla* (1914) is one such tale. Mādhava, king of Śrīhaṭṭa (Sylhet), needed his merchants to trade, so his most successful, a family of six brothers, were dispatched. The wives were distraught, especially the youngest, Campāvatī, who had just been married to the youngest brother, Jayānanda. While their mission was proving successful, Satya Pīr decided to test them: should they refuse to offer his coveted *śirṇī*, they would pay dearly. Dressed as a *faqīr*, Satya Pīr approached Jayānanda, who being inexperienced threw him out as an undeserving beggar. Satya Pīr, enraged, cursed him to lose his wife to a *yogī*. Led by Satya Pīr, a grieving *yogī*-widower made his way to Campāvatī; he sprinkled her with the Pīr's magical dust and transmogrified her into a black dog, spiriting her away to the Daṇḍaka Forest, near the city of Ijvillī. There in his hermitage he sprinkled the dog with the dew from newly bloomed flowers, and she miraculously returned to her youthful form. Comparing herself to Sītā abducted by Rāvaṇa, she enjoined the *yogī* to leave her unmolested until the completion of her twelve-year vow, whereupon she would submit. Whenever someone attempted to rescue Campāvatī—the local king and many of his courtiers and of course Jayānanda, followed by his five brothers—the *yogī* ensnared them with a magic rope and transformed them into palm trees. Intoxicated with his own prowess, the *yogī* succumbed to his own arrogance and renounced his worship of Satya Pīr, which of course was the prelude to his undoing. The faithful Campāvatī staked a claim for redress as a reward for her fidelity, so Satya Pīr privately promised her release by a member of her own family. That undoing would come in the form of Campāvatī's nephew, for the eldest son Hīrānanda had providentially impregnated his wife prior to his departure; the boy's name was Bāghāmbara.

With the predictions of greatness upon him, Bāghāmbara grew and was properly educated until he could undertake the rescue. Along the road he met the Pīr, who explained to him the new reality of his age: there is no difference between the Vedas, the Purāṇas, and the Qur'ān. To prove it, the young Bāghāmbara was granted a vision of the Pīr as the four-armed Nārāyaṇa, a vision which faded into the flute-playing Kṛṣṇa. It was this vision that seemed to give him a *carte blanche* for dealing with any kind of problem; the apparent realities separating religions and their communities were undermined, were demonstrated to be something other than what he had imagined. The Pīr blessed him and departed. Bāghāmbara soon discovered Campāvatī, who was turned to a formless lump of flesh by the touch of a silver rod when the *yogī* left each day and restored with an identical rod of gold when he returned. Bāghāmbara revived his aunt who with him conspired to discover the secret of the *yogī*'s miraculous life force, which proved to be an owl that roosted on the Isle of Laṅkā. Bāghāmbara trapped the owl and returned to Ijvillī, where, with the magic rope, he rendered the *yogī* helpless. Under duress the *yogī* restored to life the king, his courtiers, Jayānanda and his brothers, and their various valuable livestock as well. With the population liberated, Bāghāmbara then moved to kill the *yogī*, but the owl slipped his grasp and plunged into the ocean. Bāghāmbara pursued, and just as he gripped the owl, both were swallowed by a great fish. Bāghāmbara calmly petitioned Satya Nārāyaṇa, who beached the fish and split his belly; Bāghāmbara and the writhing owl were disgorged from its bowels. Bāghāmbara slew the owl, killing the *yogī*, and was awarded the daughter of the king of Ijvillī for his actions. Everyone returned to Śrīhaṭṭa, where they instituted the permanent worship of Satya Pīr.

As will be obvious to those familiar with other folk traditions, many of these tales readily yield to analyses of their common narrative elements, such as those cataloged in the Stith Thompson motif indexes (1955–58) and found in the predetermining structures of Vladimir Propp (1975). In these elements one finds an often simple, but ambiguous, morality that seems to provide an oblique social commentary, not so much to condemn but to question values that do not always lend themselves to easy application. One can even see a function not dissimilar to Bruno Bettelheim's (1988) critique of fairy tales, providing the reader with the opportunity to imagine for oneself appropriate responses to unusual and compromising situations. In these tales one predictably encounters the naive and gullible king, whose simple desires and scheming ministers or wives generate problems for the unsuspecting. Of course, there are magic wands or ropes, flying horses, and a parade of anthropomorphized talking animals. In a manner common to India—perhaps made most famous by the *Tutināma*—talking birds are especially prominent, such as those that work with the fowler in *Ākhoṭi pāla* of Rāmeśvara (1924, 1963) and as transformation vehicles for humans, as seen in the *Madanamañjarī pāla* noted above. Much of the miraculous in these tales stems from the use of magic and other arcane arts; spells and incantations abound, many of which are linked to a knowledge of esoteric Tantric texts, such as those which empowered the antagonists in Rasamaya's *Galakāṭāphyāsarā pāla* (n.d.; Miya and Stewart n.d.) and the nearly identical anonymous retelling titled *Manohāraphyāsarā pāla* (1905). These magical conjurers are often linked directly to blood sacrifices, more human than animal, as witnessed by Kṛṣṇa-śaṅkara's *Satyapīrera pāñcālī* (*Vallabha pāla*) (1862; Miya and Stewart n.d.). Ogres and witches—such as those who flew in the top of a tree each night to bacchanalian pleasures in distant lands as described by Wāzed ʿAlī (n.d.) or the bloodsucking sisters in Kiṅkara's *Śaśidhara pāla* (1914b)—were also a commonplace, often linked with the more benign weaver of magic spells, the *mālinī*. This flower vendor, whose knowledge of compelling potions, unguents, and fragrances was legendary, appeared as a common plot-twisting character in more than a half dozen tales within the cycle. The presence of these folk narrative elements, coupled with the nearly total elimination of overt religious posturing, leaves the interpreter of the religious content of the romance cycle of tales hard-pressed for explanations. In these tales, Satya Pīr is present, Satya Pīr impels the action, Satya Pīr is clearly oriented toward both Hindu and Muslim audiences; and yet the stories do not appear particularly to be about Satya Pīr or religion at all. It is no surprise, then, that academic interpreters have simply ignored these stories. The causes for this omission—largely the disjunction between method and material—can show where we might profitably realign our interpretive strategies to better read these documents.

SETTING THE PROBLEM

When Bengali literature of the precolonial and early colonial period (and this seems to apply to Indic literature in general) depicts some kind of encounter between various Hindu and Islamic communities or individuals, as in the Satya Pīr cycle, scholastic analysis approaches these texts as sociological studies rather than literature, assuming that they document directly a Bengali religious reality. At the same time, these studies all too frequently assume from their contemporary perspectives that the categories of 'Hindu' and 'Muslim' are mutually exclusive, setting up each as the extreme of otherness. In the process much of the direct and indirect evidence of the texts is ignored. In these kinds of academic studies (and certainly without making this move explicit), the categories themselves are understood to be driven by ideological commitment.[8] They are concomitantly driven by what I see as a cultural application of the Western philosophical 'law of the excluded middle' (a thinly disguised ontological move that shifts from ideology to argue that an individual cannot 'be' two things at once, a strategy that equates ideological commitment with ontological transformation). When a story within a narrative literature—or, alternately, a statement from a theological or practical manual or even some ethnographically documented cult activity (ritual)—has been shown to elide the boundaries that divide these, or other similarly opposed, categories of religious affiliation, the item in question is generally treated as something strange, unnatural, or aberrant. That seems to have been the fate of Satya Pīr; it is all too seldom that the categories of analysis are themselves brought into question. This perceived aberrance, of course, is rhetorically useful because it shifts the analysis away from the ostensible, but ultimately uncooperative, object of study—the encounter of Hindu and Muslim in a shared holy figure—in a way that reinforces the exclusion of the categories that were assumed at the outset. The most common strategy is to treat the resulting encounter as 'syncretistic' (for example, Rāya 1991; Roy 1982: 129–32, 1983: 214–18), which appears to take the resulting phenomena seriously but actually operates through metaphoric structures which invariably, but perhaps not always intentionally, imply a generally negative value judgment (Stewart and Ernst 2002).[9]

The value judgment inherent in the analysis of syncretistic entities which are projected as 'aberrant' produces another common rhetorical move that fades almost imperceptibly into the metaphor of medical 'abnormality.' Cultural and religious structures that are syncretistic can only be the product of a diseased, that is, unhealthy, malformation that, because they cannot endure, should be expected to die.[10] This negative biological and medical metaphor does have the effect, however, of inviting some kind of analysis of the objects in question because it is especially through the study of the diseased or abnormal that one finds what is normal, what is healthy, what is standard. But because the syncretistic entity is assumed to be the product of two or more healthy and normal contributors or something or someone healthy who has been diseased by the alien 'other,' the resulting analysis can only confirm what was assumed to be prior in the first place—in the example of Satya Pīr, the pristine categories of Hinduism and Islam. This, of course, is a thinly disguised but widespread version of the logical fallacy of *petitio principii*, assuming the conclusion as the starting point. Consequently, this approach does not create new knowledge of the thing in question, rather it only replicates its own beginning. In this restatement of the original thesis—that Hinduism and Islam are eternally separate entities that form exclusive religious identities—the only variable remains the degree of the judgment passed regarding the value of such formations, that is, whether the patient is potentially curable or terminally ill.

The structure of the metaphors that control these related concepts of syncretism—whether mechanistic, alchemical, biological, or medical—can become blunt instruments of interpretive torture when turned to literature. Because they uniformly propose a fixed structure, the analysis of literary narrative through the concept of syncretism can at best hope to find either fixed images that confirm and reify its assumptions (e.g., when wearing the garb of a Muslim *faqīr*, Satya Pīr manifests multiarmed forms of Vaiṣṇava divinity) or attempt to force the surface narrative through its mold to result in a crude allegorical readings (the encounter of the Pīr with a recalcitrant Hindu king, for example, who finally acquiesces to Satya Pīr's power, read as a Bengali Hinduism forced to accommodate a Muslim presence). The first two categories of Satya Pīr's literature occasionally yield such opportunities, if intermittently, but the third category of romance renders such heavy-handed readings highly suspect, as evidenced in the samples suggested above. Even the obvious examples of images which can be called syncretistic depend frequently on the interpreter's bias. For example, in the story of Bāghāmbara, Satya Pīr's manifestation of the four-armed Nārāyaṇa, followed by the two-armed Kṛṣṇa, can be read in completely opposing directions. The Pīr (representative of Islam) has at his core a higher reality of divinity (representative of Hinduism), making Islam but a manifestation of the higher truth of Hinduism. Alternately, the divinity so exalted by Vaiṣṇavas can be seen here as but one of the many powers manifested by the human Pīr of Islam, thereby diminishing the Vaiṣṇava divinity in a hierarchy of greater and lesser forms that yields to the superiority of Allāh as the sole and unique God. This ambiguity can be resolved only by choosing sides, assuming a starting point from which to interpret the whole, which of course takes us back to the fallacy indicated above. If the hierarchy of inclusion can be read in completely opposing directions with minimal effort, that ambiguity suggests that not only is syncretism itself suspect as an analytic tool but also the image in question may not at all be about a fusion of these apparently opposed viewpoints but perhaps something quite different.

If both readings are possible, then the combined religious elements in the figure of Satya Pīr might better be understood to signal a different kind of conception or activity that does not predetermine its outcome in clear ideological or religious positions. Rather, the indecisiveness itself suggests that Satya Pīr—and the world he inhabits—marks an arena within which the ways these religious traditions come together might be actively reconsidered. The very lack of fixity for any one image, and the different readings that are possible within these tales, make clear that the issues have not been fully adjudicated and finally determined but are very much in the process of negotiation or exploration. With this in mind, it becomes clear that the first cycle of tales, with their decidedly Vaiṣṇava bent, has become ossified, leaving little room for the imagination, although still partaking of the fictional narrative form; about the only room left for improvisation is in the language itself by the demonstration of poetic virtuosity. The second cycle of tales, which is nominally Muslim but considerably more ambiguous than the first, seems to pit the doctrinally secure against each other in ways that shake their foundations but ultimately yield a largely triumphant Islamic presence in a land filled with various Hindus, many of whom are to be understood as respecters of common truths. The tales of the third cycle, the romances, free themselves from overt ideological positioning—and it is precisely this withdrawal of the actively doctrinal element that signals their willingness to experiment, not to predetermine the alignment of the traditions in question. The fact that the romances push overt doctrinal formulations to the sidelines and restrain Satya Pīr himself just outside the periphery—only bringing him in to initiate the frame for the narrative or to impel the action when the protagonists are stymied—announces that these tales give a much freer play to the imagination, and with that freedom experiment with possibilities that are constrained in the more ideologically determined first two cycles. With this freedom granted by exiling those actions that are overdetermined by doctrine or theology, the romances indulge in speculation that questions the very bases upon which society—and the place of the individual within it—is constructed (cf. Laine's and Wagoner's chapters in this volume).

As literature, the romances are much more compelling than their counterparts, even though the structures of action and constituent tropes are predicated on common folk forms. But it is precisely their more truly fictional nature that makes possible an active exercise of the imagination without being wedded to socially determined consequences, that is, the greater the fiction in these narratives, the freer they are to express the improbable with impunity, to explore ideas that are otherwise limited by religious and social pressures. And in this, the romances avail themselves of typical literary forms of expression—images and impressions—to suggest their direction. It is through these imprecise media that ambiguities abound. Any place in the narrative where we can locate serious ambiguities, we have the potential for discovering the unstated points of the story, the driving issues that are being explored in the work of the imagination (the obvious parallel with Sigmund Freud's [1955] dream interpretation is certainly germane here). It is here where the firm ideological or doctrinal positions, which have been banished to the sidelines, are discretely opened to question. The romances of Satya Pīr open a discursive space within which new forms of religious interaction can be adjudicated and some of their implications pursued. Yet this is not a realm without limits. The shape of the narrative itself is still dependent on the possibilities within the discursive arena of its formation, so we must look to the nature of that discursive space in order to see what kinds of issues are being made possible by it. Our choice of foil, our representative piece and point of entry to the different romances of Satya Pīr, will be the entertaining nineteenth-century 'Tale of Lālmon.'

KAVI ĀRIPH'S *LĀLMON KĀHINĪ* OR *LĀLMON KECCHĀ*

The time was the late fifteenth century (Āriph 1866, 1868, 1984): Lālmon was the daughter of a *wazīr* who, being bereft of sons, raised his only daughter as a boy. He sent her to the local school in the king's court where she studied alongside a young prince named Ḥusayn Shāh. For years they passed the time as classmates only for Ḥusayn to discover her real gender by accident: She was brushing her hair dry after a bath when her clothing slipped down and revealed her budding breasts. Ḥusayn, struck dumb by the revelation and instantly aroused, pressed her into a marriage, but not before the quick-thinking Lālmon extracted several promises from him. As Ḥusayn in his impatience moved to consummate the nuptials, Lālmon resisted long enough to call a witness to their hasty promises, and the only witness she could muster was her spiritual guardian Satya Pīr. When Satya Pīr materialized in the room upon her call, Ḥusayn drew his sword in a frenzy against the intruder who promptly responded by cursing him to die at the hands of lowly dacoits. The mode of his death would be to lose his head, severed with an instrument fittingly like the one with which he threated Satya Pīr. At this point Lālmon's and Ḥusayn's adventures began in earnest.

Naturally enough, Lālmon and Ḥusayn were incapable of hiding their love marriage. Following the way of all palace intrigue in which secrets are seldom well kept, their liaison was discovered to the displeasure, even wrath, of their parents. About to be slain for their indiscretions, they fled. They girded themselves as warriors, with stolen swords, shields, and helmets, and then stole expensive princely stallions to make good their escape. In their haste they took a wrong turn—for as everyone knows, a curse cannot be outrun—and soon found themselves not along the familiar highway but turned back onto a byway that proved to be the nest of a particularly nasty band of highwaymen. In the thick of battle with these dacoit avengers, they belatedly recognized the hand of Satya Pīr. After vanquishing the legions of assassins in a battle where Ḥusayn and Lālmon fought in a classic back-to-back defensive position, Ḥusayn naively imagined that he had escaped the curse. But against the advice of Lālmon, he refused to slay the last standing enemy, a young and miniscule servant. This young waif bade his time until Ḥusayn had dropped his guard, and at that swift moment, the child swung his sword with a vengeance through Ḥusayn's exposed neck. In her grief, the devoted Lālmon—who was compared directly to the famous Behulā, who refused to abandon her husband Lakhīndāra when slain by a viper through the curse of the goddess Manasā (for the most popular, see Dimock 1963; Gupta 1962; Ketakādāsa 1976; Vipradāsa 1953)—cradled Ḥusayn's severed head until all of the forest's animals began to fast out of sympathy. The forest grew deathly silent and the ordinary world ground to a halt. Through the power of her devotion and impelled by the compassion shared by the wild animals, Satya Pīr gradually became alerted to her plight. From the power of her purity and intent, Lālmon was then granted a boon from Satya Pīr. To no one's surprise, she used it to restore Ḥusayn's life.

With Ḥusayn safely resurrected and order again restored to the forest, the seriousness of the couple's plight began to hit them in earnest. They had wandered into a strange and hostile land, the likes of which they had never seen; they were without friend or asylum, and they were traveling incognito—Lālmon retained her disguise as a warrior—wearing stolen royal armor and riding stolen royal stallions of a distinctive red color. Overwhelmed with hunger, for they had not eaten for days, they encamped in a grove so that Ḥusayn might slip into town to buy food. He went on foot to attract less attention, while Lālmon remained in the grove tending the horses. With a little invisible guidance by Satya Pīr, who was still not satisfied with Ḥusayn's commitment, a local Rājā stumbled on to the tethered horses and instantly took Lālmon for a horse thief, beginning another test of the couple's endurance.[11] She was quickly remanded to prison, and her horses confiscated. Meanwhile, Ḥusayn had run into more troubles of his own. As he entered the town he passed by the place of a *mālinī* who in the manner of such women was locally recognized as a witch. She spotted Ḥusayn and instantly saw in him a man of high social standing. Sensing an unusual opportunity, for he was strikingly handsome, she rearranged her hair in a more alluring fashion and fixed it with a fresh string of flowers. She sprinkled herself with perfume and reached for one of her most expensive garlands to proffer him. Overwhelmed with his handsome features, even her studied confidence began to wane, but knowing the hearts of men, she positioned herself in his way, bowing so that her clothing strategically slipped. It worked. For the second time, Ḥusayn found himself mesmerized by the charms of a woman's 'innocently revealed' pulchritude, and as his eyes riveted on the curves of the *mālinī*'s body, she slipped a garland of enchantment over his reeling head. How could he know that he had been duped, that the *mālinī* had sprinkled the garland with a magic dust, quickened with muttered *mantras*? In the twinkling of an eye Ḥusayn was ensorceled, and before he could cognize what had transpired, she had turned him into a ram or billy goat, had tethered his neck, and had led him home. There Ḥusayn was held captive—a ram by day and a charming prince by night—in order to gratify the insatiable lurid appetites of the witch among witches.

As Ḥusayn alternated between the twinned pastoral pleasures of limitless food and sex, Lālmon was unceremoniously hurled into jail without so much as an opportunity to defend herself. She understood her plight, not metaphorically but literally; she imagined her incarceration to be a karmic reward for her dreadful failure in love. Losing hope she began to fade, certain that nothing could intervene. She wasted away, for all the world another fallen warrior, rotting in the stench of his cell—for no one had discovered the secret of her gender. As she languished through the days, it came to pass that a rogue black rhino had set upon the fields of the kingdom in a rampage, threatening to destroy a full season's crops. None of the local king's warriors succeed in the slaying of the beast, so in a last ditch effort to avert disaster, the king announced a reward for slaying the animal. Miraculously Lālmon heard of it and was given a glimmer of hope. She bribed her way out of jail (why she had not done so before is not stated), and, still in the guise of a man, she tracked and then slew the awful animal, for she had the power of Satya Pīr to aid her. Other warriors quickly butchered the carcass and presented their pieces to the king, claiming the reward, but Lālmon alone had the tongue and horn. From that the king knew this warrior to be the true slayer of the deadly rhinoceros. With the carnage of his kingdom now allayed, true to his word, and in a gesture befitting the hero, the grateful king publicly made over the hand of his daughter to the as yet unnamed soldier. Everyone was aware that the king had no male offspring and was anxious to perpetuate his lineage the next best way: a son-in-law offered the opportunity. Still not having achieved her goal of recovering Ḥusayn, Lālmon chose to play along for the time being.

Lālmon had little choice but go through with the marriage, but she refused to consummate it, pleading with her distraught 'bride' that if she would indulge her for ten days, everything would be revealed and made right. Unhappy, but realizing that as a bride she had little say, Lālmon's male waited. Lālmon feverishly began to erect a mosque, now that she controlled princely resources. With that construction, Lālmon hosted an extended carnival appropriate to the event. She calculated that everyone in the kingdom would eventually hear about the entertainment and come to visit, both out of respect and of course for the food and celebration. She had figured well. Ḥusayn had heard of the new prince's construction project and suspected that it might be his beloved Lālmon, so he cajoled the witch into taking him. She was uneasy but not without compassion. She transformed him into a man, but she disguised him and bound his tongue with spells so that he could not speak. She watched him like a hawk, but when he went outside to relieve himself, he managed to write a message on the wall with the charcoal of burned tobacco. Lālmon, who had been constantly patrolling the premises on alert for signs, recognized the writing and was able to follow the lead and track him to the witch. Lālmon had the flower vendor apprehended on charges of kidnapping but, to the surprise of the guards, demanded that they bring along the ram grazing in the yard.

In the court, the puzzled king asked for an explanation, whereupon Lālmon accused the *mālinī* and then demanded she transform the ram back into her beloved. The *mālinī* tried to bluff, pointing out the futility and stupidity of such a charge, but when Lālmon drew her sword—still in her guise as a warrior—the witch relented. Ḥusayn was conjured back into this manly form and relieved of his rather ignominious fate as breeding stock. The witch was quickly executed, and her body dispatched to the sewer to become food for swine. To the completely puzzled king, Lālmon revealed her gender and her status as Ḥusayn's wife. Being a survivor, the king realized the potential for his own complete humiliation, so he quickly agreed to Lālmon's suggestion for a way to solve the vexing problems borne of his own artless rule. The solution that would allow no one to lose face, and everyone to benefit, was simple and effective: a royal *menage à trois*. Lālmon privately revealed her gender to her 'wife,' the king's daughter, who was then made over to Ḥusayn as his second wife. But to the surprise of all, she indicated that her duty was to her one and only betrothed, no matter that 'he' turned out to be a woman. So she took a vow to serve and honor Lālmon as her sole master and mate, her *svāmī*, a selfless act that enabled her to honor her father's original gift of marriage and save the family honor. The king, in return, gained a genuine prince for a son-in-law—although his heirs would not be of his own blood—and a trusted vassal for his kingdom, for with Lālmon at Ḥusayn's side, the king found two warriors, not one. Ḥusayn Shāh, whose own adolescent indiscretions initiated this tortuous set of events, inherited a different kingdom from the one he should have ruled but had lost through his own failure in propriety. At this apparently happy outcome, the prince and his two wives promulgated the worship of Satya Pīr, who, back in Mecca, received their homage with grace and benevolence.

MAKING A SPACE FOR THE TALE

While many of the tale's elements appear to be drawn from the common stock of folk narratives from around the world, the specifically South Asian selection defines not only choices that make the tale possible but, in a symbiotic relationship, also the limits of that possibility. These choices reflect the structure of the discursive space made possible by the telling. The structure of this space—its literary and indirectly its social context—can, according to a suggestion made by Jonathan Culler (1976), be recognized by four overriding literary features that shape its contours: logical presupposition, pragmatic presupposition, implied intertextuality, and explicit intertextuality. There are, of course, numerous extraliterary features that shape the possibilities for the tale, but most of those ultimately resolve as subsets of the dominant literary concerns (e.g., prevailing intellectual trends, which will find their way into the category of logical presupposition, or preferred modes of abstract discourse, which would find their way into the pragmatic presuppositions).

As the name suggests, the logical presupposition defines the logical rules of discourse and must include then such assumptions as the manner in which arguments can be made. In this case, they clearly assume the standard operations of evidence and inference common to Indic literature more generally (Potter 1963). These narratives do not participate in the explicit articulation of theology or philosophy, nor do they attempt sustained logical argument. So, for the most part, the formal dimensions of logical presupposition do not intrude—nor do they have to be accounted for—in the simple logic of the tale. But the prevailing logical presuppositions do play a major role in the assumptions regarding cosmology and the structures of the universe that dictate consequences of choice. While little is articulated explicitly, the narratives hinge on the operations of a general law of *karma*, where cause and effect do carry over, not just within a life but also across multiple lives, although that is more implied than played out in the narratives. Explanations for current events are sought through a retrospective evaluation of past action, and consequences are calculated for the future, although there is less of the latter than the former. With this assumption of the operations of *karma* comes the correlative proposition that life is somehow cyclical. Perhaps more importantly for our purposes, the arrangement of the cosmos that would support cyclical time allows for a movement of individuals through different frameworks of reality (i.e., the level of cycles), so that intercourse between humans, spirits, titans, deities, and gods or God is not only possible but also assumed to be fairly readily accessible to those who develop special powers. This, in turn, hinges on the assumption that individuals do have the ability to master secret lores that give them access to powers beyond the norm—a very important feature not only for the protagonists and antagonists but also for Satya Pīr himself. That Ḥusayn can be slain in this tale and then brought back to life through Lālmon's devotion or that he can be transmogrified into a ram and back again without any apparent ill effects, bespeaks this sort of world. It might be argued that the world so created in this narrative, and in the other romances, is a thoroughly Hindu construction that adapts an occasionally Islamic perspective to its own devices. Satya Pīr, residing in Mecca but available within an instant, speaks to the adaptation of the institution of the *pīr* to a local reading that equates it with the office of *deva* or some other celestial figure.

While the narrative operates according to these and other less compelling logical presuppositions, the shape of the narrative itself defines a choice as well, starting with genre, perhaps the most important of the pragmatic presuppositions after the choice of language. As should be obvious, the choice of the Bengali vernacular serves to unify audiences who might otherwise be divided by more overtly religious language or the poetic conceits of the languages of high culture, Persian or Sanskrit. As we have already seen, the narratives of Satya Pīr adopt a literary form that falls somewhere among a number of other popular genres, comfortably nestled between the popular *kissā* literature on one end of the spectrum and the semiepic *maṅgala kāvya* on the other. That position, with ties to a predominately Muslim and another predominately Hindu literature, suggests part of its self-definition, for it is creating a connection that does not appear to privilege either a strictly Muslim or a strictly Hindu conception of the world. Consonant with the other tales in the romance cycle, the choice of the format as it is preserved in all of the manuscripts and printed editions (totaling approximately 550 couplets unbroken into chapters or sections) is consistent with others in its genre; it is of a size and construction that lends itself either to public delivery or private consumption, while favoring neither Hindu nor Islamic forms. With no overtly religious frame, the narrative is portable, that is, it can be shared as entertainment or placed within the context of a chosen religious observance (e.g., the proffering of *śirṇī*). Its affinity with *kissā* and *pāla gāna* literatures argues for its concern to characterize, if not depict caricatures of, contemporary society, albeit indirectly. In Bengali arts and letters, this and closely related forms have often proved to be a favored vehicle for such endeavors. The exaggerations of commonly promoted values (e.g., the fidelity of women as *satī*) signal their questioning, and the situations that are created—the more bizarre, the more likely to focus the attention—become opportunities to deliver often stinging indictments of prevailing moralities or at least to bring them to question. In short, by the choice of this malleable literary form, Kavi Āriph, the author of *Lālmon kāhinī*, has predisposed his audience to hear his story in a special way; he has created an expectation that follows the form. This grants him a freedom to experiment with otherwise difficult or even taboo subjects but at the same time constrains him from taking positions that would otherwise alienate his audience and do violence to the medium. Consonant with the genres with which he has connected his work, the author may speculate and question but is effectively barred from drawing clear-cut conclusions; what resolutions emerge do so through the resolutions of plot, which as will become apparent are invariably ambiguous.

Whether self-consciously or not, Āriph further defines the arena in which his text is to be understood when he refers to other stories. He does not refer to texts by name, so there is no overt or explicit intertextuality as one often finds in more theologically or historically driven works. However, he does invoke characters of other popular narratives and by that invocation implies a text or body of texts as background to his own work. Deliberately invoking these other narratives defines in part an intended audience—those who know or know of those texts—and at the same time invites that reader or auditor into a prevailing discourse, giving the narrative a literary context that goes beyond genre and related structures, that is, beyond the pragmatic presuppositions. The intertextual references can come in many forms, but in the text of the *Lālmon kāhinī*, and in others within the cycle of Satya Pīr's romances, the references—without exception that I can find—are limited to simple allusions to unique and well-known characters. The allusion is seldom made to an explicit narrative event in which the characters participate but to the moral features of the characters and their way of responding to trial. When Āriph refers to Lālmon as 'Behulā' and Ḥusayn as 'Lakhīndāra,' the reference is to the story of the *Manasā maṅgala*, the tale in praise of the Hindu goddess of snakes. No specific narrative is mentioned by name, but it need not be because the issue is not situation specific. The compelling and differentiating twists that authors such as Ketakādāsa may use to shape their versions of the plot of the *Manasā maṅgala* are of no moment. Rather these references tend to allude to more general questions, especially of moral stature of the character and the effects of that character's moral action.

In spite of the nonspecific reference, the intended audience needs no help to draw the appropriate dimension of the analogy or its entailments. For example, the allusion has nothing to do with Manasā or serpents, for at the point in the narrative in which she is compared to Behulā, Lālmon is deep in the forest and alone in her grief, cradling the severed head of her husband; the reader implicitly understands from that comparison that just as Behulā's devotion brought her dead husband back to life, so too Lālmon can be expected to do the same. That Ḥusayn can be brought back to life is never in question because of the operating assumptions of the previously articulated cosmology that follows a basic Hindu outlook; such events can happen. That Lālmon will be successful is never in question because of the direct comparison to Behulā, whose wifely devotion revived her inappropriately slain husband. The comparison signals to the audience precisely what to expect.

That the outcome of Lālmon's effort is never in question—she will be successful in reviving her husband as the comparison with Behulā predicts—makes clear that the overall structure of the plot is not one of suspense, which means the point of the story is not to discover if Ḥusayn lives or dies or the uncovering of some other secret. What *is* at stake cannot be directly stated, for that would violate the narrative's nature as literature, that is, the tale would cease to be a fiction and would participate in another, more explicitly articulated realm of theology, doctrine, chronicle, or history. Consequently, what really serves as the subject can only be indirectly assessed, and in this particular example, we find an explicit starting point for evaluating the driving concerns by the explicit references to the characters of other narratives. These associations are broad and open ended but do begin to demarcate the shape of the issues. In this example, there are four associated figures for Lālmon: Behulā, who is Bengali-specific, and three pan-Indian Hindu characters, Sītā, Satī, and, as will become apparent, an indirect association with Pārvatī. This web of mythic and literary allusion not only contextualizes the tale but also starts to delimit the possible issues that are to be explored. That they are to be explored implies a certain imprecision and ambiguity, which provides much of the power of the narrative, that is, the tale is made attractive to and holds its audience by inviting the audience's participation—not in the plot's final resolution but in the ways the expected end is reached—and that participation can only take place in the realm of the imagination.

MAKING SPACE FOR THE IMAGINATION

The response generated by the tale (i.e., the explicit content of the individual imagination) can never be fully predicted or controlled by virtue of the nature of its action; it is always variable. But the way the imagination is stimulated and directed, and the discursive arena in which the imagination is brought into play, can to a certain extent be identified, for its action falls in the unstable and transient, and therefore elusive, space between the text (or its telling) and the reader (or its hearing). If this space is not activated by the imagination, the narrative fails, a result that makes clear the function of the imagination itself as a necessary element of the telling.[12] Precisely how the phenomenon of imagination works or at least the way we can conceptualize its happening (that is, the way the consciousness is engaged in the imaginative process) need not concern us now;[13] what is important is to suggest certain features that help to shape its action, and those in turn point the interpreter to the all-important ideological issues lurking on its fringes—the absent subject of the fiction.

The ideological concerns of fiction are elusive at best, for the very nature of fiction (because it is a 'fiction') drives the overtly ideological or doctrinal positions off-stage. The language of the narrative itself places certain limitations on what can be addressed—here it is Bengali—as do the choice of narrative style and fictive elements—in this case, traditional 'folk' tropes that rely on known genres. This writer, Kavi Āriph, in making the choices he does, is able both to create an object to be read or heard (his narrative) and at the same time to dictate the standards by which it is to be judged and interpreted (see Macherey 1978: 45). He is not working entirely in the absence of constraints, however, and his dependence on the audience's familiarity with related narratives makes clear its partially derivative character, no matter how seemingly unique or unusual the subject matter and its drama. Importantly, any literary fiction of a derivative order (as clearly evidenced by Lālmon's story) will automatically and of necessity seek a basis and pretext outside itself (as witnessed first by the intertextual and genre choices), for ultimately that outside support is the only guarantee of its own readability. While attempting to maintain the credible air of novelty, the text relies on traditions, moralities, and ideologies that have been previously inscribed and that ultimately limit its possibilities (Macherey 1978: 46–47).[14] But by maintaining the illusion that other narrative outcomes are possible—the quintessential fictive act—the very foundational values on which it rests, that is, those predetermined issues that inform its own writing, are actually brought into question. Unlike historically or doctrinally explicit writings, the move into fiction invites the reader or auditor to search for its underlying values, which can never be made explicit but only implied (with the possible exception of allegory), because of its fictive quality, that is, if it is fiction, it can only parody ideological discourse, but that parody can function to open a space wherein the reader may critique prevailing ideologies with a freedom not possible through other more explicitly determined and analytical forms of writing. Because of the fiction's indirection, the author must rely on the audience's imagination to investigate the ideological issues that lurk just outside the narrative's frame. At the same time, its fictional quality serves as a constraint, for it can only inculcate images and impressions that are necessarily vague and which must be given shape by other means. To get at this ideological realm, which is only indirectly addressed as the unspoken real subject, the interpreter can only develop concomitant strategies that figuratively throw the issues into relief, finding in their shadows the primary points of speculation. There are, of course, a myriad of possible approaches to these indirect issues, but no matter the genre, it is always safe to begin with whatever opportunity has been provided directly by the author. For Āriph's story, we shall start with the direct comparison of Lālmon to Behulā, one of the few direct intertextual references.

The first time the comparison is made, Ḥusayn has just been beheaded by the treachery of the slave whose life he spared, and Lālmon has responded in turn with an expression of grief that, as all the animals of the forest recognized, was several orders of magnitude beyond that of even the most devoted wife. Ḥusayn's death was the result of a curse generated by his own rash act of raising his sword against Satya Pīr, who had come to witness Lālmon's vows, but that curse is countered by Lālmon's devotion to Ḥusayn (and to Satya Pīr), effectively countermanding the curse with an even stronger boon by the giver of the curse. Hence the comparison with Behulā, whose devotion caused Manasā to return Lakhīndāra to life. Ḥusayn's initial transformation moves from one extreme to the other: alive, then dead, then alive again. Lālmon's character trait of supreme devotion—the devotion of a *satī*, who is willing to do whatever it takes to support her lord and husband—is directly involved in numerous additional transformations of Ḥusayn's status, signaling that the allusion to Behulā is not tangential but integral to the tale's values. When the witch transmogrifies Ḥusayn into a ram (man into ram), Lālmon's heroic effort returns him to his normal condition (ram into man). Part of that effort involves an intermediate transformation that must overcome Ḥusayn's bodily mutation and mute condition when outside the witch's home, an opportunity for which was provided by the mosque-building festival (ram into half-man into ram); and finally Lālmon forces the witch to turn him permanently back into a human (ram into man) while exposing the witch's tricks, ultimately resulting in her execution (witch into pig's food, a transformative category opposed to ram and man).

The final transformation, the execution of the garland-weaver witch at the end of the story—hardly the act of a traditional woman of the household—is in turn effected by Lālmon's own transformation, a gender change (or at least gender role change) that turns her into a warrior (woman into warrior). This gender shift is subsequently implicated in a number of unlikely escapes from equally unlikely predicaments encountered by Lālmon. She finds herself in trouble in the first place because she was educated as a man (girl into boy), until the youthful Ḥusayn, with whom she would have had no contact whatsoever without this improper educational activity and gender subterfuge, exposes this disguise and falls in lust, if not love, with her. She escapes her imminent death by assuming the dress and action of a warrior but flees like a common thief (wife into warrior). Subsequently, she is jailed as a thief and then bribes herself out of jail, still as a warrior (thief into warrior), but is rewarded with the hand of the daughter of the king, having slain the rhino as the best of all warriors (thief into hero into son-in-law/prince). Finally, while refusing to consummate her marriage (virulent warrior into impotent), she erects a mosque with accompanying festival to celebrate the betrothal (prince into cultural leader), which is corrected by the restoration of her husband and the revelation of her true gender (man into woman). Lālmon's improperly married 'wife' honors her father's mistake and devotes herself to the very image of devotion, Lālmon (princess into second wife/unconsummated).

The two basic transformations—the dead Ḥusayn brought back to life, and Ḥusayn's transmogrification into a ram—require for their correction Lālmon's personal devotion that eventually leads to her own transformation, a switch into a transvestite warrior. Each of these transformations mark significant points in the narrative where the heroine (Lālmon) must respond to extenuating circumstances. The responses are not always what one might expect; they are often larger than life and improvisational. These improvisations mark what Catherine Belsey has called moments of 'situation creativity' (1991: 363), to which we have previously alluded, an opportunity for the author to bring into question the norms of the ordinary by thrusting his characters into situations where the assumed order has been disrupted. And, as noted above, the more bizarre these challenges, the more likely the narrative to carry some kind of social critique. How the characters respond reflects directly on the real subject of the work, which in this world of cultural values is inevitably of ideological concern. While there are undoubtedly a myriad of ways to analyze these transformations, it is again the author's direct cue—that Lālmon's actions are those of Hindu devotion (Behulā, Satī, Sītā, and even Pārvatī, by virtue of Lālmon becoming a better warrior than all the men, much as Pārvatī became an ascetic)—that signifies a Hindu value set. While Sītā is more commonly invoked in these romances, suggesting a more clearly Vaiṣṇava model of womanly conduct and a position consonant with the image of Satya Pīr himself, the mix attributed to Lālmon must be accounted for. And, to account for it, we must account for Ḥusayn, for in many respects Lālmon's actions are presented as a mirror or inversion of his. For instance, Ḥusayn rushes to consummate his marriage vows taken in private and without witness, while Lālmon later refuses to consummate her vows that have been publicly proclaimed, suggesting that Ḥusayn's impatience led to impropriety, if not anticipating an actual infidelity (which subsequently proves true with the witch). Both question his sincerity, while Lālmon's consistent desire for propriety signifies her future fidelity and commitment, even though, like Ḥusayn, her motives are in question. The examples can be multiplied, so it is safe to suggest that the issues revolve not around a single actor but the pair taken together.

As his name suggests, Ḥusayn comes from a Muslim family, and his father is among the ruling elite, with Ḥusayn himself a possible future ruler, although there is no information regarding any siblings. What makes his name so common and easily identifiable as a Muslim is precisely what invokes such strong associations with the history of Islam, the martyrdom of Ḥusayn at Karbalā, which culminates with Mu'āwiyā's forces systematically dismembering the valiant Ḥusayn, ending finally with his head. The full force of Shī'ī tradition begins to take shape, and Ḥusayn's actions carry a dramatic weight that resonates strongly with ritual processes common to the community (see Ayoub 1978; Schubel 1993). The first introduction of the name Ḥusayn in the narrative simply signifies Lālmon's suitor's background and nominal Muslim status, but when he is cursed by Satya Pīr to lose his head, the significance of the name increases. When the fleeing couple find themselves in a pitched battle against the predicted dacoits, fighting against overwhelming odds, their backs pressed together for protection, the association with the historical Ḥusayn is crystallized into a vivid image of impending death. The expectation is dashed when Lālmon and Ḥusayn manage to prevail against all odds. Then with little fanfare the prediction comes to pass as the spared servant severs Ḥusayn's head from his body while he sleeps. Not only is the expectation finally satisfied, albeit somewhat delayed, but it also invites the reader to collapse events synchronically, even though they have been played out diachronically, each new action in the sequence complicating the image until the audience becomes aware of a direct association through that concatenation. Once the association is made, the audience might well be expected to leap to other associations, that is, to read or hear the transformation and action of the text synchronically as well as diachronically.

Ḥusayn is, importantly, one of the names of the great twelfth-century Ṣūfī mystic Ḥusayn ibn Manṣūr al-Ḥallāj, whose martyrdom affirmed the fidelity of his position as the speaker of 'truth'; he becomes an exemplary model of Ṣūfī commitment. One might not be inclined to make this connection with the Ḥusayn of Āriph, but for the fact that many Bengalis understand the origins of Satya Pīr to be rooted in this very same figure, the figure of 'Truth' or 'the True' (Sanskrit *satya*).[15] As an *avatāra* of Viṣṇu he is Satya Nārāyaṇa; as the manifestation of al-Ḥallāj he is Satya Pīr. The association with this Ḥusayn, while less explicit, still looms in the background for those who know their history. And the connection to historical personages is not limited to the strictly religious, for a number of stories likewise circulate regarding the connection of

Satya Pīr to the great Ḥusayn Shāh[16] (r. 1493–1519 CE). Āriph's Ḥusayn is explicitly given the name Ḥusayn Shāh. More often this association of Satya Pīr and Ḥusayn Shāh is proposed through Ḥusayn Shāh's daughter. She is also occasionally identified as Lālmon in Āriph's tale as well as in the explicitly Vaiṣṇava narrative of the Bengali poet Śaṅkarācārya (Sen 1920: 100), even though specific reference in both of these texts is vague at best. But in the same way that Āriph's direct comparison of Lālmon to Behulā invokes general images from which appropriate features can be lifted according to context, the ambiguous associations precipitated by Ḥusayn's name and actions thoroughly ground his character in an Islamic value set, most obviously Shī'ī, but Ṣūfī and regal as well.

Ḥusayn's second transformation—when he is captured and made into a ram by day, and the personal plaything of the witch by night—curiously, and indirectly, reifies his figure as a representation of Islamic mores. Having already been slain in battle, and with that connected to the martyrdom of Ḥusayn (Shī'ī mainly, but also Ṣūfī), the transmogrification of Ḥusayn into a ram adds the most fundamental underlying image of religious submission to the will of God (Arabic *aslama*): the substitution of the ram for Abraham's sacrifice, although here the images must be read synchronically to produce the image (Ḥusayn decapitated + Ḥusayn as a ram + Ḥusayn does not die). While Ḥusayn ultimately prevails by inheriting part of the kingdom of Lālmon's 'wife's' father in the makeshift adjustment at the end of the narrative, his depiction is not altogether sanguine, nor particularly complimentary. If he does somehow represent or at least invoke images of Islamic values and rule, the message is ambivalent, for he is brash and rash, allows his personal passions to cloud his judgment, fails to heed sound advice, becomes a thief in order to save himself, is easily seduced and duped, and comes to rule only through the efforts of others. Yet rule he eventually does, and with Lālmon, his warrior-wife, and a second, meeker wife—one might even characterize her as the epitome of submissiveness—by his side. Is it too much to start to see a mild allegory developing with this Ḥusayn (allegorically representing some kind of Islam) cohabiting with a devoted Lālmon (allegorically Vaiṣṇava, but ultimately representing a wider range of Hindu ideals), ruling over a submissive populace, pawns in their game?

If the allegory holds on this most general level (the level of association and suggestion) which is most likely given the nature of the genre, then Lālmon's dramatic manifestations of worldly potency and her accompanying gender subterfuges make her an ambiguous figure at best. For these traits, when evaluated collectively, fly in the face of her portrayal as the perfection of devotion, *satī*. Only one figure is transparently clear: the other female, the witch, is unambiguously scheming and conniving, the antiheroine. Her unmitigated self-centeredness and unbounded lust tend to deflect attention from the ambiguities in Lālmon's character, largely because of the sympathies Lālmon has generated through her tireless devotion, which even resurrected her dead husband. As the antithesis of devotion, the voluptuous garland weaver, who ensorcels the hapless Ḥusayn and reduces him to a gigolo (the ram is an especially appropriate form here), gains her power through the spells and potions of an arcane magic. While garland weavers are traditionally associated with lover's potions, and all that follows from their unique intermediary position as an aid in the quests for love, the ability to transform humans into animals, to mesmerize the unsuspecting into vulnerable positions, and to master the alchemy of the nether regions, takes one far from the role of duenna and go-between into the arena of a blacker magic. That mastery is an arcane and mysterious expertise that falls within the purview of Tantrics and yogins (and a few Ṣūfī masters as well),[17] and it is self-serving and oriented to power in this world, as opposed to some future world. The shameless bestiality of the garland-weaving *mālinī*, whose love-making activities are not for anyone's good but her own, provides a compelling inversion of the image of the *gopī*-loving Kṛṣṇa, who likewise mesmerizes and conquers members of the opposite sex—but in that Vaiṣṇava system glorified and hailed as the key to everyone's salvation. And with this recognition, the disjunctions of Lālmon's double-identities suddenly come more clearly into focus, for the loving wife (a benign image of a Vaiṣṇava devotion and submission) has personally vanquished the *mālinī*, beating her at her own game, forcing the witch to reverse her magic, and, ultimately, decapitating her (a terrifyingly vengeful image of feminine power, much like Durgā or even Kālī). Lālmon's power proved superior, overwhelming the *mālinī*, who only selfishly dabbled around the fringes of this magic for her limited gain, while Lālmon plumbed its very depths. That Lālmon would prevail few readers would doubt, but the reason for this expectation is that Lālmon had already demonstrated an absolute power over mortality itself; she had resurrected her decapitated husband. And that power is unique for it stretches to the absolute limits of what is characterized in South Asia as *tantrika*.

It is this suspected Tantric connection that accounts for much of the uneasiness that pervades Lālmon's character, for the dominant side of her dogged devotion is not one of gentle submission no matter the affront to her dignity or the awkwardness of her position (as her own 'wife' so easily accepted at the end of the narrative) but one of female dominance and the exercise of a world-shaping power. It is no surprise, then, that the image of Sītā (the long-suffering heroine) is virtually absent in this narrative (unlike others) and actually more appropriately attached to the submissive second wife, while the images invoked directly in the text for Lālmon are the active images of *śakti*: Pārvatī and Satī and, of course, Behulā. And it is again the explicit image of Behulā that makes clear that the comparison to Lālmon is an allegorical clue. For Behulā, long regarded as the image of wifely devotion—a standard that prevails to this day in Bengal, no matter the religious orientation—makes her devotion reap rewards not just by being pure and good but also in fact by flouting convention and subverting the normal order, by practicing the most esoteric forms of Tantra.[18] When her husband Lakhīndāra dies, his body is not cremated but floated down the river as is custom in Bengal.[19] But Behulā goes a step further by refusing to abandon her husband; she floats down the river with him. Alternately holding him on her lap (a Bengali euphemism for sexual intercourse) or straddling him (an explicit image of sex), she floats beyond the ends of the earth to the land of the gods, where by the intervention of Śiva, who shames Manasā into aiding her own devotee, Behulā receives the boon that restores Ḥusayn's life. Śiva's intervention on Behulā's behalf unravels the nature of her action, for it is this same Śiva to whom Tantric practitioners direct their energies when they perform their austerities in the cremation grounds. Behulā is not just a devoted wife, she is performing *śava sādhana*, the ritual worship of a corpse for purposes of attaining immortality, power over death, in this case her husband's. Her actions mirror this *sādhana* or *pūjā* as described in Āgamavāgīśa Kṛṣṇānanda's Sanskrit *Bṛhattantrasāra* (1984: especially 438–45), a compendium of Tantric ritual that has been extremely popular in Bengal since the eighteenth century (see also Banerji 1978). In general outline, the severity of her ascesis (*tapasyā*) compares only to that of *yoginī*s, a term that in Bengali not only designates female adepts in the esoteric reaches of *yoga* but also a witch who has control over the darker forces. The point is that while it was Behulā's absolute devotion to her husband that precipitated her action, the power that actually restored his life was the arcane magic derived of Tantric ritual. And Lālmon does the very same. Refusing to bury her husband, as would be customary, she sits in the forest cradling his severed head, the severity of her passion finally radiating through the forest until the entire animal world is brought to a standstill, and those wild animals are so impelled by her *tapasyā* that they collectively fast with her, multiplying her power. Finally that power touches Satya Pīr in Mecca, the same figure who had levied the curse in the first place. He is forced to find a way to counter it, moved by Lālmon's love and devotion to her husband but coerced by her Tantric power. Lālmon triumphed over death in this world, but the power that enabled her to do so runs directly counter to the positive powers associated with the virtuous and proper. Lālmon, like Behulā before her, presents a double-sided, and, therefore, ambivalent, image of feminine power; one benign and tranquil, the other violent, aggressive, and potentially disruptive and threatening. And were there any question about the nature and source of this power, it is Lālmon who, out of devotion to her husband, beheads and desecrates the witch. The act leaving the impression of a triumph over the Tantric element (in this case associated with evil) but actually through an act of blood sacrifice, a much greater practice of the Śākta's craft, whose power Lālmon controls absolutely.

CONCLUSION

This ambiguity in Lālmon's character complicates the simple allegorical suggestions with which we first began to unravel the elusive issues being explored by this narrative. A reading that would follow traditional syncretistic interpretations would lead to a heavy-handed labeling of characters that would uncomplicate the narrative and, at the same time, grossly underestimate the amount of ambiguity by having to ignore many important elements of the tale. By isolating the discursive arenas in which the tale operates, the author provides clues to the reading of his text. But the effect of his narrative is not to champion a particular position, as would be expected in a doctrinally or ideologically driven narrative, but to bring to light some of the incredible complexity with which actors must deal in a world whose populations must negotiate different kinds of power articulated through different modes of religious action and belief. Cosmologically, the narrative does not distinguish between a general Islamic and a Hindu universe, rather melding the former into the latter in a unified system. Where they differ is in the realm of their action and the domains of their powers, but those are more precisely delineated in this narrative than the categories of Hindu and Muslim would allow. Rather the narrative makes clear that distinctions must be made on a finer level than these broad characterizations that have dominated the nineteenth- and twentieth-century discourse on the relation of the religions. Satya Pīr is not a Hindu and Muslim figure, rather, in this case, he is a figure who represents an alliance and working relationship among Vaiṣṇava and Shīʿī or to a lesser extent Vaiṣṇava and Ṣūfī. If the images invoked by the narrative represent in any way the religious traditions—and it is clear by now that they do create those associations, however unsystematically—then the course of the narrative's action raises serious questions about the viability of such an alliance, about public posturing, and displays of martial power versus the private manipulation of powers unseen. Similarly, the traditional gender roles are severely questioned, pointing to the very dangerous power of women and the ways that they control men and function in a complex world order that shifts the hierarchies of power depending on the level and situation. But, ultimately, Lālmon's tale—and even more so in the context of other romances of Satya Pīr—invites the audience to consider the way that a masculine-oriented world order, created and maintained by ruling Muslims (in government), might counter its extreme opposite (in theology and action), a *śakti*-driven Tantric subversion, dominated by females and fueled by blood sacrifice. In some sense this opposition to Śaiva and Śākta is mediated through the ruling alliance with Vaiṣṇavism, which in its Bengali form champions a discrete control of the feminine while vitally recognizing its power, something that forms of South Asian Islam have historically found difficult. What Āriph did was to compose a narrative that raised the questions, not stipulate answers, and the continued popularity of his tale bears witness to its power to give play to the imagination, to wonder 'what if'? In the world he constructs, the balance of power is demonstrably unstable and dynamic, while the recognition of what constitutes the truly other that aligns Shī'ī and Ṣūfī with Vaiṣṇava in stark opposition to Śaiva and Śākta marks a different, more profound divide in ways of working in the world than the political divisions that a syncretistic reading would propose. Kavi Āriph's world is not exclusive, neither seeking nor proposing the separation of its many actors, but demonstrates the complexity of different forms of power with which people must content. And, in the process, it suggests that Satya Pīr and the alliance he represents is but another player in a world far more contingent than one envisioned as simply Hindu or simply Muslim.

Notes

1. This literature is second only to that dedicated to the religious figure Kṛṣṇa Caitanya. I have located more than 750 extant manuscripts in various repositories in West Bengal, India, Bangladesh, and London, UK; for the most complete listing of manuscripts, see Bhattacharjee (1978). No fewer than 160 different printed texts have been circulated since the mid-nineteenth century, probably considerably more. Altogether, I have found more than 160 authors who have composed texts in honor of Satya Pīr.

2. The most popular of these tales are by the medieval Bengali poets, Rāmeśvara and Śaṅkarācārya, whose texts can be found in numerous printed editions; for example, Śaṅkarācārya and Rāmeśvara (n.d.a, n.d.b, 1952). For translations of samples from these tales, see Stewart (1995), which includes selections from Śaṅkarācārya, Dvīja Rāmabhadra, Bhāratacandra Rāya, and Ayodhyārāma Kavicandra Rāya. The tale of the merchant occasionally constitutes an independent work and may represent a discrete subgenre of its own; for example, Kavivallabha (1914); Sena (1928).

3. The most extended narrative and arguably the most entertaining of all of the tales is the quasi-hagiographical account of this mythic figure in Kṛṣṇaharidāsa (n.d.). For additional stories of this type, including a summary of the contents of the aforementioned text, and accounts of other mythic and historical *pīrs*, see Girīndranāthadāsa (1975).

4. For an extended analysis of these two strains of the literature, see Stewart 2000. This chapter also includes an extensive bibliographic survey of those two styles of texts. In other forms of this 'crossover' literature, the tendencies are reversed, with Ṣūfī and other texts routinely appropriating Vaiṣṇava and more general Hindu cosmologies; see for example numerous of the texts included in Śarīpha (1969). See also suggestions on how to interpret these complex constructions in Stewart (2001).

5. For surveys of the former, see Sen (1920); see also Pāla (n.d.); the histories of Bengali literature by Asit Kumāra Bandyopādhyāya, Aḥmad Śarīpha, D. C. Sen, and Sukumar Sen. For a detailed study of the romantic literature and its connection in Bengal, see Ṭarafdār (1971); for the Bengali side of this connection, see also Aḥmad (1970). The *kissā* literature stretches in one form or another across northern India; see Pritchett (1985).

6. Another version of this text is by Karṇa (n.d.).

7. The test was to uncover her private parts to gauge her response.

8. An epistemological move that in the eyes of postcolonial theorists is the inescapable result of the pervasiveness of the Protestant privileging of intellectual commitment over praxis in the history of the study of religion, which has been dominated by those same Western intellectual interests.

9. As Ernst and I have demonstrated, all the models of syncretism—including 'influence,' 'borrowing,' 'cultural veneer,' 'miscegenation,' 'hybridization,' and 'alchemy'—are predicated on metaphoric constructs that ultimately imply that the thing being created is somehow unnatural, its parts brought together in some unholy alliance that ensures that the entity will not endure, cannot reproduce itself, or at least will disaggregate in future generations.

10. The ubiquity of this metaphor makes it at times nearly invisible, but it stretches back certainly as far as Max Müller's 'disease of language' as an operative construct in the analysis of South Asian religions (1897; see also 1870, 1871, especially volume 2).

11. Of course she really was a horse thief, no matter where the sympathies of reader may lie.

12. Among the forms of reception esthetics—starting with that initiated by Hans Robert Jauss at the University of Konstanz—it is reader-response criticism that, while refining certain propositions of deconstruction, has greatly enhanced our understanding of the role the reader plays in creating the text. The text of course becomes a variable entity based on what the reader brings to it and how he or she understands it. There is an obvious debt here to basic hermeneutic theory, such as Gadamer's (1985). Of special interest is the approach adopted by Iser (1974, 1978) and Rabinowitz (1987); see also the very useful anthology edited by Tompkins (1980).

13. While closely related to the reception aesthetic, this is the proper domain

of literary phenomenology, perhaps the most significant theorist of which was Poulet; see his 'Criticism and the Experience of Interiority' (1980), which is reprinted, although heavily edited, in Tompkins.

14. For Macherey, the author's freedom is in no sense indiscriminate but conditioned by the factors that limit the creation of the text in the first place, especially the traditions, the moralities, and the ideologies that shape the intellectual context of a text's writing.

15. This popular story can be found in the preface to Kavivallabha (1914: 7). This connection is repeated frequently, although never with traceable citation, generally treated as 'hearsay.' The strongest argument for the connection can be found in Massignon (1975, 2: 299–302).

16. Whose benevolent reign in Bengal stretched for more than twenty-five years, a period marked by a tremendous religious tolerance (coinciding with the period of the life of the Vaiṣṇava figure Kṛṣṇa Caitanya) and a stimulation of arts and letters, accounting for many of the great original works and translations of the middle period of Bengali literature (see Mukhopādhyāya 1980: especially chapter 7; Tarafdar 1965).

17. See, for instance, the unpublished work of Carl Ernst on the *Amṛtakuṇḍa*, a Persian translation of a Sanskrit text circulated among Ṣūfīs and containing Nātha and other yogic formulae for enhancing sexual prowess, bringing women under control.

18. Although I have never seen this openly acknowledged by any scholar or teller of the tale.

19. The poison works on the body in much the same way as fire, but it is hoped by the bereaved that the waters of the river might cool down the burning poison and, more importantly, the body might float by some *ojhā*, a handler of snakes and master of poisons, who might administer an antidote and revive the dying or dead.

References Cited

Aḥmad, Oyākil. 1970. *Bāṃlā romanṭika praṇayopādhyāna*. Ḍhākā: Khān Brādārs eyāṇḍ kompāni.

'Alī, Munśī' Wāzed Ṣāḥib. N.d. *Madanakāmadevera pāla: Satya pīrera pūthi*. Ḍhākā: Moḥammad Solemān.

Anonymous. 1905. *Manohāraphyāsarā pāla: Satyanārāyaṇa pāñcālī*. Kā̃thai: Nihara Press.

Āriph, Kavi. 1866. *Lālamonera kecchā*. Kalikātā: Sudhānidhi Yantra.

Āriph, Kavi. 1868. *Lālamonera kecchā*. Kalikātā: Viśvambhara Lāha.

Āriph, Kavi. 1984. *Lālamonera kāhinī* (ed. Girīndranāthadāsa). Gokulapura, 24

Parganās: Śrīmati Karuṇāmayīdāsa.

Ayoub, Mahmoud. 1978. *Redemptive Suffering in Islam: A Study in the Devotional Aspect of 'Ashura' in Twelver Shi'ism.* The Hague: Mouton.

Banerji, S. C. 1978. *Tantra in Bengal: A Study in its Origin, Development, and Influence.* Calcutta: Naya Prokash.

Belsey, Catherine. 1991. "Constructing the Subject: Deconstructing the Text." *In* Robyn R. Warhol and Diane Price Herndl, eds., *Feminisms: An Anthology of Literary Theory and Criticism*, 593–609. New Brunswick, N.J.: Rutgers University Press.

Bettelheim, Bruno. 1988. *The Uses of Enchantment: The Meaning and Importance of Fairy Tales.* New York: Vintage Books.

Bhattacharjee, Jatindra Mohan. 1978. *Catalogus Catalogorum of Bengali Manuscripts.* Point 1. Calcutta: The Asiatic Society.

Chakraborty, Usha D. 1963. *Conditions of Bengali Women around the Second Half of the Nineteenth Century.* Calcutta: Bardhan.

Culler, Jonathan. 1976. "Presupposition and Intertextuality." *Modern Language Notes* 91: 1380–96.

Dimock, Edward C., Jr. 1963. "The *Manasā-maṅgala* of Ketakā Dāsa: Behulā and Lakhīndār." *In* Edward C. Dimock, *The Thief of Love*, 195–294. Chicago: University of Chicago Press.

Freud, Sigmund. 1955 [1899]. *The Interpretation of Dreams* (trans. James Strachey). New York: Basic Books.

Gadamer, Hans-Georg. 1985. *Truth and Method.* New York: Crossroads.

Gayārāma. 1926. *Madanamañjarī pāla: Satyanārāyaṇa pāñcālī.* Khā̃tai: Madhusudhana Jana at Nihara Press.

Girīndranāthadāsa. 1975. *Bāṅglā pīra sāhityera kathā.* Kājīpāḍā, Bārāsāta, 24 Paraganās: Śehid Lāibrerī.

Gupta, Vijaya. 1962. *Padmā purāṇa* (ed. Jayantakumāra Dāsagupta). Kalikātā: Calcutta University Press.

Inden, Ronald. 1976. *Marriage and Rank in Bengali Culture.* Berkeley: University of California Press.

Iser, Wolfgang. 1974. *The Implied Reader.* Baltimore: Johns Hopkins University Press.

Iser, Wolfgang. 1978. *The Act of Reading: A Theory of Aesthetic Response.* Baltimore: Johns Hopkins University Press.

Karṇa. N.d. *Madanasundara pāla.* Cuttack: H. M. Duttā at Dutta Press.

Kavibara, Dvīja. 1914. *Bāghāmbarera pāla: Satyanārāyaṇera pāñcālī.* Khā̃tai: Midnapura at Nihara Press.

Kavivallabha. 1914. *Satyanārāyaṇa pūthi* (ed. Munśī Abdul Karīm). Kalikātā: Baṅgīya Sāhitya Pariṣat by Rāmakamala Siṃha.

Ketakādāsa, Kṣemānanda. 1976. *Manasā maṅgala* (ed. Akṣayakumāra Kayāla).

Kalikātā: Rākhāla Sena.

Kiṅkara[dāsa]. 1914a. *Matilālera pāla: Satyanārāyaṇera pāñcālī*. Khā̃tai: Midnapura at Nihara Press.

Kiṅkara[dāsa]. 1914b. *Śaśidhara pāla: Satyanārāyaṇa pāñcālī*. Khā̃tai: Madhusudana Jāna at Nihara Press.

Kiṅkara[dāsa]. 1923. *Rambhāvatī pāla: Satyanārāyaṇa pāñcālī*. Khā̃tai: Madhusadana Jāna at Nihara Press.

Kṛṣṇānanda, Āgamavāgīśa. 1984. *Bṛhattantrasāra* (ed. Rasikamohana Caṭṭopādhyāya, with Bengali Translation by Candrakumāra Tarkālaṃkara). Kalikātā: Navabhārata Publishers.

Kṛṣṇaharidāsa. N.d. *Baḍa satya pīra o sandhyāvatī kaṇyāra pūthi*. Kalikātā: Nurūddin Aḥmad at Gāosiya Lāibrerī.

Kṛṣṇaśaṅkara. 1862. *Satyapīrera pāñcālī*. Ḍhākā: Dhaka University Bengali manuscript 59-C.

Macherey, Pierre. 1978 [1966]. *A Theory of Literary Production* (trans. Geoffrey Wall). New York: Routledge.

Massignon, Louis. 1975. *La passion de Husayn Ibn Mansûr Hallâj*. 2 vols. Paris: Gallimard.

Miya, Shah Jahan, and Tony K. Stewart, eds. N.d. *Satya pīrer pāñca pūthi: Bikalpita kāhinīra aitihya*. Ḍhākā: Sāhitya Patrikā.

Mukhopādhyāya, Sukhamaya. 1980. *Bāṃlāra itihāsera dū'śo bachara: Svādhīna sulatānadera āmala (1338–1538)*. Kalikātā: Bhāratī Book Stall.

Müller, Fredrich Max. 1870. *Lectures on the Science of Language*. 2 vols. New York: Charles Scribner.

Müller, Fredrich Max. 1871. *Chips from a German Workshop*. 3 vols. New York: Charles Scribner.

Müller, Fredrich Max. 1897. *Introduction to the Science of Religion*. London: Longmans, Green and Co.

Pāla, Praphulla Candra. N.d. [1958]. *Prācīna kavioyālāra gāna*. Kalikātā: Kalikātā Viśvavidyālaya.

Potter, Karl H. 1963. *Presuppositions of India's Philosophies*. Westport: Greenwood Press.

Poulet, George. 1980. "Criticism and the Experience of Interiority." *In* Jane Tompkins, ed., *Reader-Response Criticism: From Formalism to Post-structuralism*, 41–49. Baltimore: Johns Hopkins University Press.

Pritchett, Francis W. 1985. *Marvelous Encounters: Folk Romances in Urdu and Hindi*. Delhi: Manohar.

Propp, Vladimir. 1975. *Morphology of the Folktale*. Austin: University of Texas Press.

Rabinowitz, Peter J. 1987. *Before Reading: Narrative Conventions and the Politics of Interpretation*. Ithaca: Cornell University Press.

Rāmeśvara. 1924. *Ākhoṭi pāla: Satyanārāyaṇa pāñcālī*. Khā̃tāi: Madhusudana Jāna at Nihara Press.

Rāmeśvara. 1963. *Ākhoṭi pāla*. *In* Pañcānana Cakravartī, ed., *Rāmeśvara racanāvalī*, 536–49. Kalikātā: Baṅgīya Sāhitya Pariṣat.

Rasamaya. N.d. *Galakāṭāphyāsarā pāla*. Ḍhākā: Dhaka University Bengali manuscript 214.

Rāya, Kānāi Lāla. 1991. "Satyapīr." *Bāṃlā Ekāḍemī patrikā* 36, 2: 71–82.

Roy, Asim. 1982. "The Pīr Tradition: A Case Study in Islamic Syncretism in Traditional Bengal." *In* Fred W. Clothey, ed., *Images of Man: Religion and Historical Process in South Asia*, 112–34. Madras: New Era Publications.

Roy, Asim. 1983. *The Islamic Syncretistic Traditions of Bengal*. Princeton: Princeton University Press.

Śaṅkarācārya, and Rāmeśvara. 1952. *Śrīśrīsatyanārāyaṇera pā̃cālī: Līlāvatī kalāvatī daridra brāhmaṇera upākhyāna* (*pūjādravya pūjāvidhi, dhyāna o praṇāma sambalita*) (comp. and ed. Avināśacandra Mukhopādhyāya; rev. Surendranātha Bhaṭṭācārya). Kalikātā: Kalikātā Tāūn Lāibrerī by Kārttika Candra Dhara.

Śaṅkarācārya, and Rāmeśvara. N.d.a. *Śrīśrīsatyanārāyaṇera pā̃cālī: Līlāvatī kalāvatī daridra brāhmaṇera upākhyāna*. Kalikātā: Tārācā̃da Dāsa and Sons.

Śaṅkarācārya, and Rāmeśvara. N.d.b. *Śrīśrīsatyanārāyaṇera pā̃cālī: Līlāvatī kalāvatī daridra brāhmaṇera kāhinī* (*pūjādravādi o pūjāvidhi sambalita*) (ed. Gaurāṅgasundara Bhaṭṭācārya). Kalikātā: Rājendra Lāibrerī.

Śarīpha, Aḥmad, ed. and comp. 1969. *Bāṅlāra sūphī sāhitya: Ālocanā o nayakhāni grantha sambalita*. Ḍhākā: Bāṃlā Ekāḍemī.

Schubel, Vernon James. 1993. *Religious Performance in Contemporary Islam: Shi'ī Devotional Rituals in South Asia*. Columbia: University of South Carolina Press.

Sen, Dineshcandra. 1920. *The Folk Literature of Bengal*. Calcutta: Calcutta University Press.

Sena, Lālā Jayakṛṣṇa. 1928. *Harilālā* (ed. Dīneśacandra Sena and Basantarañjana Rāya). Kalikātā: Calcutta University.

Stewart, Tony K. 1995. "Satya Pīr: Muslim Holy Man and Hindu God." *In* Donald S. Lopez, Jr., ed., *Religions of India in Practice*, 578–97. Princeton: Princeton University Press.

Stewart, Tony K. 2000. "Alternate Structures of Authority: Satya Pār on the Frontiers of Bengal." *In* David Gilmartin and Bruce B. Lawrence, eds., *Beyond Turk and Hindu: Shaping Islamicate Identities in South Asia*, 21–54. Gainesville: University of Florida Press.

Stewart, Tony K. 2001. "In Search of Equivalence: Conceiving Muslim-Hindu Encounter Through Translation Theory." *History of Religions* 40, 3: 260–87.

Stewart, Tony K., and Carl Ernst. 2002. "Syncretism." *In* Peter Claus, Sarah

Diamond, and Margaret Mills, eds., *South Asian Folklore: An Encyclopedia.* New York: Routledge.

Tarafdar, Momtazar Rahman. 1965. *Husain Shahi Bengal, 1494–1538 AD: A Socio-Political Study.* Dacca: Asiatic Society of Pakistan.

Ṭarafdār, Momtaẓar Raḥmān. 1971. *Bāṃlā romanṭika akāvyera āoyādhī-hindī paṭbhūmi.* Ḍhākā: Bāṃlā o saṃskṛta vibhāga, Ḍhākā Viśvavidyālaya.

Thompson, Stith. 1955–58. *Motif Index of Folk-Literature: A Classification of Narrative Elements in Folktales, Ballads, Myths, Fables, Mediaeval Romances, Exempla, Fablaux, Jest-books, and Local Legends.* Copenhagen: Rosenkilde and Bagger.

Tompkins, Jane P., ed. 1980. *Reader-Response Criticism: From Formalism to Post-structuralism.* Baltimore: Johns Hopkins University Press.

Vipradāsa. 1953. *Manasā-vijaya* (ed. Sukumar Sen). Kalikātā: Asiatic Society.

The *dharma* of Islam and the *dīn* of Hinduism: Hindus and Muslims in the Age of Śivājī

James W. Laine

The broad, almost obsessive interest that many contemporary scholars have for the theme of identity has entailed a companion concern, a concern of 'difference.' In speaking of 'them,' 'we' define ourselves and draw the boundaries accordingly. With respect to South Asia, the historical definition of Hindus by a powerful Muslim minority as 'other' is one instance of this massive contemporary cultural and scholarly interest in the theme of identity. We must see ourselves as immersed in this 'identity project' and recognize the ideology it silently presupposes while remaining open to the lessons learned in the continuing discussions of multiculturalism and identity politics. Similarly, there are some dominant models for understanding religious communities of Hindus and Muslims that produce a sort of knowledge that replicates contemporary patterns of identity construction and occludes real insight into premodern identities. This replication occurs among modern communalists who read history teleologically, finding in the past all the ingredients for a future subcontinent divided into two or more political states by religion. In this scenario, the world of the Hindu is radically separate from the world of the Muslim, and their religions are the single definitive factor in separating them. The replication also occurs among modern secularists. They find in the past a world where religious differences are mere style, encompassed by an all-inclusive universalism. They applaud not only the likes of Kabīr[1] but also celebrate the pragmatic villager who embraces nothing but particulars, uncorrupted by the claims of literate, partisan theologians. The villager is affably rustic at home with people and practices only superficially colored by the cosmopolitan religions of Hinduism and Islam.

If I try, in my current discussion, to avoid these master narratives, do I have another story to *tell*, with its own plot, heroes and villains, beginning and conclusion? Yes, in the sense that I see in the texts I examine an emergent discourse, a narrative of identity which imaginative people construct through processes of selection and repression. Conversely the answer may also be no, in the sense that I find in these texts no obvious telos, no assumed conclusion to which they all point. Rather, I find the voices of a range of contestants with varying competing interests who push the boundaries of identity, including and excluding in a variety of ways consonant with their own concerns.

All portrayals of Hindu-Muslim relations may depend in part on a picture of two clearly differentiated communities. Not only do I want to dispute the accuracy of such a representation, I want to further complicate our image of premodern Hindu and Muslim relations by showing that Muslim or Hindu self-identification through differentiation was often very different from the way their coreligionists from different classes and social locations might identify themselves. Moreover, I want to show that the very categories employed in these reflections on identity—'Hindu,' 'Muslim', '*dharma*,' '*dīn*,' 'religion'—were manipulated and modified by the individual Muslim or Hindu who used them. To anticipate my argument (the word 'religion' is often taken to mean 'a whole way of life' for premoderns but describes a more circumscribed ideology and organization for moderns), I will argue that the definition and understanding of this particular category was not univocal for premodern Indians but was employed with a range of broad and narrow definitions.

I want to consider one further framing issue before pursuing the substance of my argument: How one defines otherness and difference. I have already stated that in speaking of a group of people as 'other,' the in-group is working to define itself. Jonathan Smith (1992) has shown that this process is not simple and that one should distinguish between strategies that portray the out-group as *different* but comprehensible and strategies that emphasize the *otherness* or unintelligible alienness of the barbarian: ' "otherness" blocks language and conceptualization; "difference" invites negotiation and intellection' (p.10). This is, I believe, a useful distinction and correlates with two strategies employed by religious groups in their evaluation of other religious communities: (*i*) exclusivism as a strategy of 'othering,' and (*ii*) inclusivism as a strategy of understanding difference (Hacker 1957, 1983; Halbfass 1983; Oberhammer 1983). The exclusivists claim an authority for their religion and its theology and practices. They also see other religions as misguided rivals, in need of radical correction; the out-group is incomprehensible, barbaric, wrong. The inclusivists, on the other hand, see some validity and truth to the other's position and work to include that position within their broader framework. They, therefore, 'tolerantly' affirm the other's views and practices, even while relativizing them within a ranking system which they, sometimes rather quietly, authorize.

One might be tempted to accept a simple view that portrays the Islamic perspective as exclusivist and the Hindu as inclusivist. According to the rather abstract stereotype, the Muslim is the missionary, bearing a final revelation which claims authority over, and submission from, all persons. According classical Islamic doctrine, in primordial times all persons were drawn from the loins of Adam and asked to make submission (*islām*) to God ('Am I not Your God?'). Here on earth, in history, they must simply remember this original pledge. This would seem to be classic exclusivism. Inclusivism, a term coined to characterize Hinduism (Hacker 1983), does indeed seem to suit a tradition which includes and ranks religious persuasions, just as it includes and ranks the array of castes which constitute society. But this portrayal, which replicates some of the tropes of Orientalism and Neo-Hinduism and is more theological than historical or anthropological, ignores the data that disturb the tranquillity of doctrinal descriptions.

First, Brāhmaṇa *literati* did indeed adopt an inclusivist strategy in interpreting the caste system. They buttressed its self-evidence with the doctrine of rebirth and produced hierarchized philosophical analyses (e.g., the *Sarvadarśanasaṃgraha*) or theorized the relative powers of popular deities. But these same intellectuals, when confronted with Islam, continued to write far more in the way of critiques of long-vanquished Buddhism (different but not 'other') than they did of the religion of their political and military masters. Their silence and intellectual disinterest in Islam, as a religion and set of ideas, suggests the strategy of othering and excluding than distinguishing and including.

Second, whereas Hindu polytheism and iconophily might provoke revulsion in some Muslims, in practice most Muslims found it far more effective to include their Hindu subjects as followers of a legitimate alternative religion than to repress them as idolaters. The usual strategy was to group Hindus in the category of 'People of the Book' (*ahl al-Kitāb*) like Jews, Christians, and Zoroastrians: monotheists whose originally pure monotheism had been corrupted but were nonetheless tolerable and comprehensible. Having declared Hindu belief to be utterly different from Islam, Abū Rayḥān al-Bīrūnī then reverses himself and declares well-educated Hindus to be true monotheists:

> The Hindus believe with regard to God that he is one, eternal, without beginning and end, acting by free-will, almighty, all-wise, living, giving life, ruling, preserving; one who in his sovereignty is unique, beyond all likeness and unlikeness, and that he does not resemble anything nor does anything resemble him (1973: 17).

One notes in this statement of approbation that Al-Bīrūnī ascribes to Hindus several orthodox Islamic theological positions he might find lacking in many Muslims.[2]

Given the limits of my own scholarly expertise, I approach the question of Hindu otherness not from the perspective of Muslim authors othering Hindus but as apperceived in Maharashtrian Hindu texts, in which Hindus defend themselves, construct apologies, and attempt thinking in new·categories. I consider the world in which Hindus and Muslims interacted in seventeenth- and eighteenth-century Maharashtra to see what ways of constructing identity and otherness were available to people in that time and region.

KINGSHIP: RELIGION AND POWER

We begin with issues of kingship, since the popular view holds Śivājī Bhosle (1627–80) to be a 'Hindu' king who founded a Marāṭhā kingdom that resisted Muslim hegemony and kindled a revival of Hinduism. I will interrogate the narrative of Śivājī's Hindu kingship with two questions: (1) what did Śivājī see himself as doing? (assuming that he had an identity and that this identity presumed a sort of autobiographical reflection), and (2) what did others see Śivājī as doing?

Śivājī began his political career as the *jāgīrdār* of Pune, a position assigned to him as a boy by his father Śāhajī, who was employed by the ʿĀdil Shāh of Bijapur as a prominent general and governor of Bangalore. Śivājī began his career 'within the system' of ʿĀdil Shāhī, one of several Muslim Sulṭānates vying for power in the Deccan. All the rival Sulṭāns of that period necessarily courted powerful Hindu chiefs, who styled themselves 'Rājās' and thought of themselves as both feudatory Kṣatriyas and servants of Muslim Shāhs. Śivājī's grandfather Mālojī and father Śāhajī were successful soldiers and governors as the direct result of their service to a series of Muslim rulers (including the Niẓām Shāh of Ahmednagar and the ʿĀdil Shāh). His maternal grandfather Lakhojī Jādhav allied with the Mughuls. Reading history teleologically, later writers who glorified Śivājī saw in his father a would-be Hindu revivalist constrained by circumstance to tolerate Muslim overlordship while waiting for a realistic chance at *svarāj*. Thus, he was delighted to see his son succeed in just that enterprise. Śāhajī's contemporaries, however, would probably have seen him as the grateful beneficiary of his Muslim patrons. At his death, he passed his extensive South Indian possessions not to Śivājī but to Śivājī's half-brother Ekojī, the founder of the Bhosle lineage of Marāṭhā Rājās of Thanjavur. Śivājī was sent to Pune as a boy, accompanied by Śāhajī's first wife, Jijābāī, to administer a completely undeveloped region. Thus, he was left to gain his own political and military power by the force of his own will and skill. Continually testing the limits of actual ʿĀdil Shāhī (and later Mughul) power, Śivājī slowly established his own control over much of Maharashtra, culminating in his dramatic claim of authority as Hindu Mahārājā over this realm in a revived orthodox coronation ceremony in 1674. In short, whereas Śivājī's powerful relatives (grandfathers, father, half-brother) were Hindus and Rājās who accepted Muslim patronage, Śivājī himself began to fashion a novel narrative of legitimacy for his 'Hindu' kingship. He did so (1) by having himself declared a true Kṣatriya (a fact disputed by many Maharashtrian Brāhmaṇas); (2) by being crowned Chatrapati in an orthodox ceremony; and, (3) by commissioning literary works in Hindi and Sanskrit which not only praised him for his heroism but also argued for his genealogical purity and royalty. In a sense, then, he 'othered' himself.

We receive hints of the ways in which these different perspectives were voiced during his early career from a variety of sources. We have, for example, a recounting of a dispute between Śivājī and the More (Maurya?) clan who controlled the district of Javli (near Mahableshwar) until 1656. The dispute occurred when Śivājī forcibly annexed the region. A chronicle of the More family declares the Mores as legitimate rulers by the grace of a local god, Mahābaleśvara (a version of Śiva), as mediated through the authority of the ʿĀdil Shāh:

> We are the kings of the Konkan [Maharashtrian coastal plain]; our king is Shri Mahabaleshwar. By his grace, we rule. By his grace, the Padshah was pleased to give us the title 'Raje' and the morchel and the throne (cited in Patwardhan and Rawlinson 1929: 70).

Similarly, the *Śivabhārata* (3.5–7, 5.11–13), a Sanskrit text Śivājī commissioned at the time of his coronation, legitimizes his father's service to the Niẓām Shāh and his later rule in South India as servant to the ʿĀdil Shāh. In such cases, then, Hindu kingship subsumed under Muslim dictatorship is seen as perfectly reasonable by both Hindus and Muslims. Presumably, the Hindus in these settings fully participated in Islamicate military and courtly life, different in religion but not 'other,' encompassed but not excluded. It is worth noting here that Śivājī's grandfather Mālojī arranged the marriage of his son Śāhajī to Śivājī's future mother Jijābāī by winning the Niẓām Shāh's support for the union despite the aristocratic objections of Jijābāī's family (Citnis 1924: 20). Thus, in a dispute between two Hindu Rājās of different social standing, the Muslim emperor could assume the authority to arbitrate and, in hindsight, permanently alter the status of the Bhosle clan.

Against this mode of understanding, according to which the Hindu prince pragmatically rules as part of an Islamicate system, Śivājī is often portrayed as the restive rebel, discontent with compromise, and ambitious enough to seek full independence. According to such a view, Śivājī and his Muslim opponents viewed each other as *other*, not as players in a comprehensible game of pragmatic power relations. One sees this view in the *Śivabhārata*, where Śivājī's court-poet Paramānanda portrayed him as a king of kings and upholder of *dharma* against the ravages of Muslim barbarians in their attack on gods, Brāhmaṇas, and cows. Moreover, Paramānanda had to assume a very uneasy position, praising his patron Śivājī as a great Hindu king (and denigrating his Muslim opponents as demonic) while at the same time describing the rise of Śivājī's ancestors[3] in such a way that their collusion with Muslim power is excused and even accepted. Thus, while Paramānanda 'others' Muslims as demons in some cases, he fully naturalizes them in others. As we see below, depending on context, Paramānanda portrays Muslims as forces of *dharma* as well as embodiments of *adharma*.

Sheldon Pollock (1993) has argued that the use of the *Rāmāyaṇa* for political purposes, especially for portraying invading Turks in the 1150–1350 period, was in part the result of the text's depiction of the 'other' as demonic. In other words, if Turks represented a wholly different and unassimilable way of life, surely demonizing them as latter-day Rāvaṇas was an effective imaginative device for theorizing incommensurate, rival worlds at war. By way of contrast, though Rāma/Rāvaṇa imagery is not completely absent from the imaginative portrayal of Śivājī, it is *Mahābhārata* imagery, with its more subtle notions of *dharma*'s war with *adharma*, which was used more often. This seems to suggest the more complex seventeenth-century situation in which, for rhetorical purposes especially, Muslims might be seen as foreign, demonic, and adharmic but might also be recognized as quite ordinary characters in the social world. Thus otherness and difference, exclusion and inclusion, oscillate as options for representing Muslims and Islamicate power. A Muslim opponent might be a Rāvaṇa figure; more likely, he was Duryodhana. Ashis Nandy (1998) has recently argued that epic violence is violence between intimates, and he compares the Mahābhārata war between cousins to the bloodletting of the 1947 partition. Perhaps the seventeenth-century Kulturkampf was not dissimilar.

The first clue to this description in the *Śivabhārata* is the fact that the author describes his text as a '*Bhārata*'(1.22). He goes on to describe a feud among related Hindu Rājās at the court of the Niẓām Shāh (*Śivabhārata* 3). This is a family quarrel, Hindu versus Hindu, which leads to a split between two sides of Śivājī's ancestral clan and is explicitly compared to the disagreement between Yudhiṣṭhira and Duryodhana (*Śivabhārata* 5.1–2). Moreover, in these several cantos, the service of Śivājī's forebears (grandfather, father, greatuncles, uncles) to Muslim Sulṭāns (especially to the Niẓām Shāh of Ahmednagar) is seen as completely natural and even praiseworthy. To quote an example:

Whatever enemies did arise
[To oppose] the Niẓām Shāh—
Mighty Mālojī opposed them all!

So, too, did Viṭhojī (Śivājī's great uncle),
Showing the courage of Indra,
Ever do the Niẓām's bidding,
Having become his ally.

Though many were the Niẓām's friends
Still above them all stood Mālojī (*Śivabhārata* 1.167–69; my translation).

In the following more striking example, Śāhajī, fighting for the 'Ādil Shāh against Hindu Rājās in South India, is praised as one spreading the justice of Rāmarājya!:

Conquering Kēraḷa and Karṇāṭaka,
Śāhajī, a man of rough deeds,
Then filled the 'Ādil Shāh's treasury
And caused great happiness.

Having subdued other Rājās
By means of his policies
He made the kingdom of 'Ādil Shāh
Like that ruled by Lord Rāma himself (*Śivabhārata* 5.19–20; my translation).

We may note that Mālojī (having entered the Islamicate world of the Niẓām's court) named his sons for the Ṣūfī Pīr who blessed his wife with pregnancy; called on the Niẓām to support his claim of a marriage alliance with Lakhojī; and, was buried, like his brother Viṭhojī, in a completely Islamicate tomb in Ellora.

While the *Śivabhārata* is surprisingly accurate in its description of the actual collaboration between the Marāṭhā chiefs (Śivājī's family in particular) and the Sulṭāns of the Deccan, when Paramānanda turns to Śivājī himself, he describes him as an independent Hindu king at war with Muslims.

He does take pains, however, to excuse Śāhajī for his reluctance to engage in revolutionary resistance. He does this by employing the literary device of a dream during which Śāhajī receives a vision of Lord Śiva who informs him that his son is an *avatāra* of Viṣṇu, descended to Mother Earth to relieve her burdens of demonic depredation. Given this fact, he is to quell his own eagerness to rebel and to wait patiently for his son to lead the fight against Islamic oppression

(*Śivabhārata* 10.5–20).

Once Śivājī takes on the mythic role of defender of *dharma*, his rebellion against the Sulṭāns assumes the character of a Purāṇic struggle. All Muslims become incarnations of *asuras* (*Śivabhārata* 18.37–38), and Awrangzīb is said to be a demon who had accrued considerable power due to his performance of terrible *tapas* (austerities) in a previous life (9.14–18).

The definitive tale of the Śivājī legend is the story of his encounter with Afẓal Khān, a Bijapuri general always described in demonic terms (huge, powerful, cruel, iconoclastic). Afẓal is sent to subdue the annoying upstart Śivājī. Although Śivājī had sent letters to the Sulṭān arguing his continued allegiance and claiming his military activities were loyal, his conquering of several regional hill forts and annexation of several districts were clearly seen as a bid for power. Afẓal was sent with an army of 12,000 men to either defeat Śivājī or assure his true obedience to the Shāh. In the earliest ballad commemorating the event, the poet (one Agrindāsa) has Afẓal scoff at Śivājī's pretensions, especially his erection of luxurious tents in the imperial style: 'You are the son of a peasant, but your tents are decorated in *bādshāhī* style!' (Keḷkar 1961: 18v28). In other words, Śivājī should be accepting his status as servant to the 'Ādil Shāh rather than emphasizing his own royal status. The problem is not his alien religion, it is his unwillingness to play by the rules of the Islamicate political system.

Most accounts begin, however, with a description of Afẓal Khān accepting his task at the court of the Shāh in Bijapur. He marches out with his troops, making side trips to Pandharpur and Wai to 'smash idols' and harass Brāhmaṇas. He sends envoys to Śivājī demanding his submission, and they negotiate the terms of a diplomatic meeting. Forewarned, however, by his patron goddess Bhavānī, whose temple Afẓal had destroyed, Śivājī expects danger and comes to the meeting with thin chain mail under his shirt and concealed weapons up his sleeve. When Afẓal attempts to assassinate him, the young Śivājī responds quickly, killing Afẓal and leading his troops to a surprise victory.

Since Śivājī is always portrayed in this tale as the instrument of the goddess, the killing of Afẓal becomes a kind of ritual sacrifice (Laine 1995: 1–14). In one account, the goddess asks him to kill Afẓal in these words: 'A goat with thirty-two teeth has come for slaughter!' (Keḷkar 1961: 11v10). In other accounts, he beheads Afẓal and brings the head back to the goddess (Keḷkar 1961: 6)—or even to his own mother (Nānivḍekar 1959)—as a grisly trophy.

This singular act of daring, occurring in 1659, early in Śivājī's career, confirmed his reputation as a hero. Seen as an early step on the path to the establishment of an independent Marāṭhā kingdom, it is also perceived as a 'Hindu' defeat of a Muslim, despite the fact that Afẓal's army had many Hindus and Śivājī's many Muslims. In the rhetoric of the narrative, even in early seventeenth-century accounts, the Muslim is the demonic enemy of gods, Brāhmaṇas, and cows. *A Hindu narrative of realism, describing difference, gives way to a timeless account of otherness.* Glimpsed more obliquely, the view of a Muslim general like Afẓal shifts from a pragmatic alliance with Hindu soldiers like Śāhajī (as well as with those in his own army) to a religious crusade against the rebel Śivājī and his patron goddess.

Another legend associated with Śivājī's reign provides further evidence of the imagery of otherness. In a ballad commemorating the Marāṭhā defense of the fort of Simhagad in 1670 (Keḷkar 1928: 31–63; Laine 1996: 99–101), the fort's Mughul captain Udebhān embodies all those characteristics of demonic otherness. He is gluttonous, feasting on half a cow a day. He is lustful, abed with eighteen women when his fort is attacked (and uninterested in leaving bed even though his sons are engaged in mortal combat). He is wantonly cruel, not only 'sacrificing' a pregnant cow before entering the fray but also killing his eighteen women (presumably in order to prevent them from falling into the hands of his opponents).

As an epic hero opposing demonic otherness, Śivājī incarnates the sort of Rāma image Pollock (1993: 287) describes as typical of the Hindu king in the Muslim era. In literature describing Śivājī, however, this image is rarely employed. The Maharashtrian saint Rāmadāsa, a Rāma devotee often said to be Śivājī's *guru*, did write a Marathi version of the Rāma story, but this does not bear significantly upon the popular understanding of Śivājī as revealed in the numerous texts that praise his rule.[4] Awrangzīb is seen as a Rāvaṇa figure, but also as Duryodhana and others, a sort of general figure of evil oppression.

In early literature, Śivājī is a more successful hero—more an Arjuna or even Bhīma, than a divine incarnation like Rāma. Like Arjuna, he is portrayed as a 'Hindu' deeply affected by the characteristically 'Hindu' inclination to renunciation. Whereas the seventeenth-century texts emphasize his martial prowess (Laine 1995) and his classical role as protector and refuge (*Śivabhārata* 31.17–23), later texts (from 1780 onwards) portray him as a reluctant hero, given to meditation, vegetarianism, and pious devotion to Vaiṣṇava saints, especially Rāmadāsa (cf. *Santavijaya* 4.23ff.; Laine 1995: 14–17). By the period 1780–1810, accounts of Śivājī's heroism in defeating Mughul and ʿĀdil Shāhī opponents, as well as rival Maharashtrian Hindu Rājās, give way to stories which articulate the qualities of Hindu identity, an identity understood in terms of the universalistic Vaiṣṇava *bhakti* of Pandharpur. This can be seen especially in the writings of the hagiographer Mahīpati and the chronicler Citnis. This *bhakti*, associated with the god Viṭhobā and a lineage of poet-saints, Jñāneśvara and Tukārāma, has a narrative of its own that turns all of Maharashtra in prayerful inclination toward Pandharpur (cf. Karve 1988). Given the political importance of Śivājī, it is perhaps inevitable that the patriotic and the devotional narratives would merge into one story of regional identity. In this story, Śivājī is not only a Hindu in opposition to the other (to Islam), he is also a Hindu in a self-reflexive way. This eighteenth-century narrative of Hinduism no longer assigns him a particular role (one interdependent role among many, the role of royal protector and necessarily violent Kṣatriya) but, as the clear precursor of communalist universalism, sees all Hindus as having the same role, as *bhaktas*. This unrealized religious vision has all Hindus worship the one God, be vegetarians, and, in large measure, adopt the values of *saṃnyāsins*. In imagining a common opposition to the cultural threat posed by Muslims, these writers try to create a Hinduism structurally similar to Islam. Thus, regardless of what Śivājī actually accomplished as soldier and king, his court poet glorified him as a true Kṣatriya with royal blood that linked him to the Lunar and Solar dynasties—a protector of gods, Brāhmaṇas, and cows. This image was modified a century after his death, by a portrayal of the king not as a sacrificer-protector-patron but as a saint. In the first movement, Hinduism as Hinduism is undefined; there is, rather, an assumed world (*dharma*) opposed by alien forces (*adharma*). Oddly enough, in this framework, Islam can be understood as either an instance of the eternal threat of disorder or, more realistically, as one more element in an already complex and hierarchical system. Only with the portrayal of Śivājī as a would-be renouncer, we see the first steps toward a definition of Hinduism. In this, Hinduism is not a system of interdependent castes but a common faith whose followers revere peace, selfless devotion to God, and dispassionate detachment. *Bhakti* here makes the attempt to essentialize the diversity of classical Hinduism.

Ironically, in order for Hindus to oppose themselves fully to Islam, Hinduism had to be conceived as a unified faith similar to Islam. The oppositions and 'othering' characteristic of identity politics can take place in the context of a common culture. Indeed perhaps they must.

CONVERSION: CROSSING RELIGIOUS BOUNDARIES

Folk religion is all-inclusive, and at this level of religious culture we find many examples of Hindus adopting Muslim practices and vice versa. In such a world, one is Hindu or Muslim ascriptively as a matter of birth. One may nonetheless revere the saints of the other tradition, fear its gods or spirits, or quite comfortably participate in its practices. All without ever considering the possibility of 'conversion'—an idea that depends upon an understanding of religion as a matter of choice and conscious adoption. One interesting case is the poet Shaykh Muḥammad who, though known as a devotee of the Hindu god Viṭhobā, nonetheless thought of himself as a Muslim, as an inescapable fact of his birth: 'I may be *avindha* ['unpierced'], but in my heart is Govinda'[5] (cited in Ḍhere 1994: 77).

We have little data on the precise processes by which Islam became the religion of indigenous South Asian populations. In examining the case of Bengal, where large numbers converted to Islam, Richard Eaton (1993: 113ff.) has critiqued the usual hypotheses offered for explaining conversions of Hindus to Islam. He examines 'four conventional theories of Islamization in India': (1) the Immigration theory, which sees Muslim populations in South Asia as the result of migrations; (2) the Religion of the Sword theory, which sees the conversion of Hindus as the result of military force; (3) the Religion of Patronage theory, which holds that Hindus began to see it in their professional interest to convert; and, (4) the Religion of Social Liberation theory, which holds that egalitarian Islam held out hopes of a better life to those of lower castes, and they converted accordingly.

Eaton shows the weaknesses of each of these arguments, and, although his concern is Bengal,[6] we see that none of these theories account for the conversion of large numbers of Maharashtrians to Islam. We might note again that the upper classes could advance their careers and gain the Sulṭān's patronage without converting. No one was forced at sword point to convert, and immigrants were few. As for the fourth possibility, whatever Islam's egalitarian and populist ideals and theology, in fact, Indian-born Muslims remained a group fully separate from foreign-born, Persian-speaking Muslims (Persians, Turks, Afghanis). Islamicate culture in India was aristocratic and hierarchical.

From the few accounts of conversion that we do have, it is clear that for Maharashtrians 'becoming a Muslim' was an act of social transformation, a matter of leaving one's social group for another, rather than a commitment to a new theological position. And social identity is marked on the body—Muslims have unpierced ears, while Hindus are uncircumcised. These body markers are more noteworthy to seventeenth- and eighteenth-century Maharashtrians than varieties of creed. Śivājī's own generalissimo, Netājī Pālkar, once arrested by the Mughuls in 1667, decides to convert and, according to the *'Ālamgīrnāma*, is accepted by the 'faith-promoting, truth-loving Emperor [Awrangzīb]' (Sarkar 1978: 155). He is rewarded with gifts and a position in the Mughul army. He is circumcised and takes the name of Muḥammad Qūlī, and as a sign that his decision is not an individual one, he urged to have his wives converted as well. Eleven years later he 'reconverts to Hinduism' by undergoing the rite of *prāyaścitta* (expiation). Seen from the Muslim point of view, Netājī's conversion to Islam is simply a recognition of the truth and a return to the obedience once professed to the Creator in primordial time. The 'faith-promoting, truth-loving Emperor' must accept him into the fold. From the Hindu point of view, he is not so much welcomed back with 'reconversion' but allowed to undergo ritual expiation for an act of defilement. *Prāyaścitta* is a Sanskrit word for purification, expiation, and restoration of ritual status (Kane 1973, 4: 57ff.). It is discussed in *Manusmṛti* (chapter 11) as an antidote to various sins. To use the word to mean simply 'reconversion' obscures the way Hindu identity was first understood, that is, as a given, as a matter of ritual status and caste. The very idea of conversion, even reconversion, to Hinduism requires the development of belonging to a religion, as one does to a club, as a conscious act of choice. This may have been a possibility in the seventeenth century, but a word like *prāyaścitta* would clearly have retained its primary connotations. Thus, from the Muslim point of view, Netājī was different, but not other, and could become a Muslim through conversion because, in terms of Islamic anthropology, he was primordially and essentially a Muslim already. From the Hindu point of view, on the other hand, conversion to Islam is not really a possibility; Netājī's identity was fixed by birth as a matter of blood, not belief, and his return to Hinduism was a cleansing rather than a change of membership.

Another intriguing account of conversion comes from Mahīpati, writing in the late eighteenth century (cf. Ernst 1992: 35–36). In his *Bhaktavijaya*, Mahīpati writes of a Brāhmaṇa in Paithan, Bahirambhaṭ (or Bahira Jātaveda), who decides that conversion to Islam will be the ultimate act of renunciation:

> If ... I go straight away into the forest, they will bring me back through the influence of others. Still I must plan that my relations with my own caste [*svajāti*] should break....
>
> Bahirambhat then went to the house of a *Kazi* (Muhammadan priest) and he spoke very humbly to him saying, 'Take me into your caste. Your *Shastras* speak of making a Hindu into a Muhammadan [*hindū cā avindha karitā*] as a holy thing to do. Therefore do not hesitate and make me like yourself.' The *Kazi*... replied, 'Why have you become indifferent to-day? Why have you a sudden change of mind? I will help you out of [your] difficulty. You are a learned *pandit*. Why do you wish to come into our caste? (*Bhaktavijaya* 44.19–20, 24–27; Abbott's and Godbole's translation 1995, 2: 146, 147).

Here we have a *qāẓī* who, like Bahirambhaṭ, speaks of his religious group as a caste community, a *jāti*. He is puzzled and reluctant. After hesitating, he does proceed to convert Bahirambhaṭ by circumcising him, described in the text as being *bhraṣṭavile* (defiled). So, again, converting to Islam here is the equivalent of losing caste or entering a lower caste. Later Bahirambhaṭ regrets his decision and finds himself between communities, marked as a Muslim by his circumcision but also marked as a Hindu by his pierced ears. Again, it is a matter of caste and body that is determinative here, not creed. Perhaps even *prāyaścitta* will not restore him; he declares:

> [to the Muslims]
> How is it you made me a Muhammadan? See now the marks of piercing still appear in my ears.
>
> [but to the Hindus]
> You gave me a penance [*prāyaścitta*] and made me a Brahman again. ... As the foreskin which they cut [or circumcised] has not come back through the penance I have taken, how is it that I have become pure by applying to it cowdung and holy ashes? (*Bhaktavijaya* 44.52, 57–58; Abbott's and Godbole's translation 1995, 2: 149, 150).

Bahirambhaṭ is who he is, not because of what he believes or affirms but because of the body he inhabits. His flesh reveals the very stuff of which he is made. In classical terms, if he is a Brāhmaṇa, then that will be revealed in the fact of sattvic preponderance in his physical body (*prakṛti*). In such a view, conversion is not really a possibility.

THE *DHARMA* OF ISLAM AND THE *DĪN* OF HINDUISM

As suggested by much of the material surveyed above, words or categories like 'Hinduism,' 'Islam,' 'religion,' '*dharma*,' and '*dīn*' have ideologically determined variable definitions, and the scope of each word varies considerably according to the interests of its user.

The word '*dharma*' has an especially fluid meaning, dating back to early Buddhism. In its classical usage it means something like natural law, shading over to the duties of different persons in different situations. Buddhists used the word to refer to the Buddha's essential teachings, presumably the same truths for all people in all times and places, but the Buddhist emperor Aśoka (fl. 250 BCE) may have meant something quite vague by the word, something like righteousness. In the *Śivabhārata*, we find the word '*dharma*' used in two different ways. The first corresponds to the classical sense of natural law or order. In this sense, Śivājī is a divinely directed instrument of order, on a military quest to check the forces of disorder or *adharma*. In such a scheme, Muslims are incarnations of *asura*s, the agents of adharmic chaos:

> Enemies of gods and Brāhmaṇas

Demons allied with most evil Time
Who help evil and hurt the good
The causes of devastation
Descended to the earth
Disguised as barbarians (*mlecchas*) (*Śivabhārata* 5.27–28; my translation).

One effect of this mythic frame is to render Muslim rule understandable in Hindu terms; Paramānanda goes so far as to attribute the power of the Mughul emperor to the *tapas* he amassed as an ascetic demon in a former life!:

In this world, the glorious Mughul king
Will be very hard to conquer
. . . .
Long ago this evil king performed
Acts of great self-mortification.
So long as he is protected
By the power of those acts,
So long will he continue
To escape final destruction (*Śivabhārata* 9.14–18; my translation).

Paramānanda even has Muslims identifying with their role as (Hindu) demons. For example, in sending Afẓal Khān into battle, 'Ādil Shāh tells him: 'You are like a second Kali Yuga. The enemy of gods, Brāhmaṇas, and cows!' (*Śivabhārata* 17.2; my translation). This serves to include Muslims, even while demonizing them, within a hierarchy defined by classical Hinduism. Thus, one can see forces of *adharma* in the world which appear ascendant; they are temporary and will be overcome. Some Hindus may prosper under Muslim rule (cf. *Śivabhārata* 5.31),[7] but at a higher level, Muslim rule only brings the chaos of *adharma*.

If Muslim rule is to be seen as a Kali Yuga ascendance of *adharma* and all Muslims as reincarnations of demons, what then are we to make of a description in the same text of the Niẓām Shāh as a *dharmātmā* ('man of piety')? Moreover, what are we to make of the references to Islam as a 'foreign religion' or 'another *dharma*' parallel to Hindu *dharma*? In *Śivabhārata*, lamenting his father's arrest, Śivājī says, 'If Maḥmūd ['Ādil Shāh] by his own religion (*svena dharmeṇa*) does not free our great father, then he will taste the fruits of his action' (13.40; my translation). Here Paramānanda admits the legitimacy of Maḥmūd 'Ādil Shāh's 'own religion' as a guide to ethical action but, nonetheless, subjects him to 'real *dharma*,' that is, the law of *karma*. So here in one verse we have both understandings of the word '*dharma*'—'religion' or 'interpretation of reality' and 'natural law' or 'reality itself.' There are further examples of the two meanings for the word '*dharma*':

(1) Afẓal states that Śivājī is so devoted to 'his own religion' (*sva dharma*) that he destroys the 'religion of foreigners' (*mleccha dharma*) (*Śivabhārata* 17.12). Elsewhere he says that Śivājī has 'assumed leadership of his own religion' (*nija dharma dhurīṇo*) (*Śivabhārata* 19.30; my translation).

(2) Afẓal later writes Śivājī a letter in which he not only accuses him of wrongfully seizing Candra More's demesne in Javli but also of destroying mosques (*mahāsiddhinilayāḥ*, aurally evoking the Arabic *masjid*), oppressing Muslim scholars (*yavanācāryān*), and obstructing the Islamic path (*aviddhānām adhvānam*) (*Śivabhārata* 18.47ff.).[8]

(3) Similarly Śivājī laments:

All these clans of Muslims
Are incarnations of demons
Who have risen up to flood the earth
With their own religion (*Śivabhārata* 18.37; my translation).

It is clear from these passages that *sva dharma* (= *nija dharma*) cannot mean 'caste duty' as it does in the *Mahābhārata*. It means 'one's own religion,' an understanding of *dharma* as religion, path, and interpretation of reality rather than the natural law of reality itself. Thus the use of the word '*dharma*' in the frame myth of gods and demons contrasts with its meaning in the context of a Kulturkampf between Hindu *dharma* and Muslim *dharma*. In the first case, *dharma* versus *adharma*; in the second, one *dharma* versus another *dharma*. The reality of the historical situation demands some recognition that a Muslim might act according to the dictates of his own religion (as in *Śivabhārata* 13.40, quoted above) or even be virtuously pious, *dharmātmā*, while, on the other hand, the classical dualistic mythology encompasses Muslims into a *dharma* which is all reality and not one interpretation of it. In such a frame, Muslims are not allowed an authentic voice and agreeably ascribe to themselves the stereotypical roles of Kali Yuga forces of disorder. The employment of the word '*dharma*' to suggest both these meanings signifies that the classical meaning of the word '*dharma*' was, in a complicated way, in competition with an emergent concept of *dharma* as 'religion,' and 'religion' in the modern, reified, and communalist sense.

If Hindus could use the word '*dharma*' to both exclude and include Muslims in a variety of ways, we also have indications of a similar Muslim ambiva lence. In a series of letters written by the Sulṭāns of Bijapur to Śāhajī, and then to his son Ekojī, we see that the 'Ādil Shāh presumes his allies share his concern for the glory of Islam. For example, 'Alī 'Ādil Shāh II, writing in 1660, declares:

> Yekoji [Ekojī] Bhonsle, be exalted by our royal favour and know that the constant aim of His Majesty is to spread the faith of the Sayyid among Prophets (Muhammad), therefore the breeze of victory has always blown in the banners of my generals. The proof of it is that at this time the infidel wretch and rebel Shiva [Śivājī] had raised his head in tumult and shown the utmost audacity. Therefore, ... [Siddi] Jauhar Salabhat Khan was sent by us with an army and officers to root out that infidel rebel. When the general marched out for uprooting that impure *kafir*, the wretch feeling himself unable to confront the Islamic army, turned his face toward flight, and the army of unbelievers that had gathered around him like wild dogs, dispersed in different directions. The army of Islam is in pursuit of him, and by the grace of God will in short time either make him a captive or destroy him.
>
> You should, on hearing this glad news, offer thanks to the undiminished fortune of his Majesty (cited in Sarkar 1978: 76).

So, again, here in the same text, the Sulṭān can presume that the Hindu Ekojī can rejoice in the victories of the 'army of Islam' over the infidel. Somehow, since Ekojī was a loyal ally, unlike his half-brother Śivājī, that meant that he shared in the Islamic mission, even though he was Hindu. Śivājī, on the other hand, was both not Muslim and in opposition to Islam. Thus he can be castigated as *kāfir* (infidel) and leader of the army of unbelievers. And when Śāhajī dies, the Sulṭān offers Ekojī consolation: 'We hear that our son the Maharaja has left this world for the eternal above' (cited in Sarkar 1978: 80). This may be formulaic, but it is a rather unthinking inclusion of a Hindu into an Islamic afterlife.

To return to Hindu portrayals of Muslims, I should mention that except for the rare usage of the term '*mleccha*' for 'Muslim,' the usual term in Sanskrit is '*yavana*' or 'Greek.' This is a sort of timeless category meaning 'foreigners from the northwest' and might not include the Siddis or Abyssinians who are often (but not always) considered separately. We also find the words 'Paṭhān' and '*aviddha*' (unpierced, Marathi *avindha*), but we never find the word 'Musalmān,' as we do in Marathi texts of the same period. Again, the use of the vague, classical designation *yavana* serves to encompass Muslims within a Sanskritic worldview, whereas the Marathi vernacular, heavily Persianized in the seventeenth century, readily incorporated terms and concepts natural to Muslims and better suggests the Islamicate tincture to the courtly life of that time. In the earliest of Marathi ballads, a song that celebrates Śivājī's killing of Afẓal Khān, Śivājī is called 'Sarjā,' a Persian word for lion; Muslims are called Musalmān; Śivājī 'sends his *salām* to his father' and is described as dressing in Islamicate fashion. In this text, the city of Pune is famous for the *dargāhs* (tombs) of Ṣūfī saints (*Śivabhārata* 4; Keḷkar 1928: 8). The text itself has so much Persian vocabulary as to make it unreadable for most modern Marathi speakers.

Given that the word '*dharma*' is used to render the English word 'religion,' it may not surprise us to find a reference to 'Hinduism' in Persian as *Hindo dīn.* In a Persian text purported to be Śivājī's letter to Jay Singh, we have a militant statement of the opposition of Hinduism to Islam as rival religions or, in Islamicate usage, rival *dīns* (Sardesai 1927: 172ff.). In this text, Śivājī is writing to his fellow Hindu, the Rājpūt and Mughul captain Jay Singh, who marched to the Deccan in 1665 with a large army, hoping to gain Śivājī as an ally in a Mughul campaign against the 'Ādil Shāh a year after Śāhajī's death. After a long endeavor, Jay Singh secured Śivājī's submission and alliance, leading to Śivājī's fateful visit to Agra to the court of Awrangzīb in 1666. Whether the letter is authentic, it is a fascinating statement of Hindu self-understanding through Persian and Islamic categories. In short, the complex diversity of religious belief and practice, which early Muslim arrivals to India saw as a multitude of sects and communities (Ernst 1992: 22ff.), was now a unity, a religion, a *dīn*. On the other hand, Awrangzīb and the oppressive Mughuls were 'Rakshasas in the guise of men, devoid of justice and religion (*dīn*), and sinful' (Sardesai 1927: 173v19). Śivājī asks Jay Singh to join him to attack these 'enemies of religion' (Sardesai 1927: 174v31). He laments, 'Had Darashikoh been king of this country, he would have treated his people with kindness and favour' (Sardesai 1927: 174v32), suggesting that not all Muslims or Mughuls were necessarily demonic.

CONCLUSION

In seventeenth- and eighteenth-century Maharashtra, questions of religious identity[9] involved complicated answers. Some might claim Hindu identity and ascribe to others a Muslim identity primarily as a matter of birth. Others, admittedly, a smaller group, might consider religious identity a matter of creedal allegiance. For the majority group, conversion from one religion to another is impossible, unthinkable, or, at least, extremely peculiar. For a minority of people, the modern idea of religion is now a possibility: people can choose a religion as a matter of individual conscience. According to this view, it is incumbent upon righteous Muslims to welcome Hindus into the fold. Hindus who think in this way are able to conceive of Hinduism as a religious persuasion as well as an ascriptive group, even if they would not usually convert Muslims.[10] In a sense, however, a Muslim can be converted to the Hindu doctrine of inclusivism and begin to recognize their faith as one among many. They can then, like Dārā Shikūh or the Niẓām Shāh, be cheered as just and righteous, as dharmic.

In seeing the variety of ways Hindus and Muslims viewed each other—as other or as different—it seems safe to conclude that most Hindus and Muslims viewed those followers of other religions as quite natural members of their social world and 'othered' them as demonic and incomprehensible more as a rhetorical act than as a sociopolitical act. Even differences are sometimes unconsciously forgotten, and Hindus are welcomed into an Islamic heaven or Muslims granted yogic powers. Because Hindu society was premised on the idea of difference and hierarchy (and thus presumed that difference would be negotiated in social, political, military, and even religious contexts) most Hindus accepted Muslims as different but not other. Muslims, too, who had largely accommodated themselves to the same social world, did the same. For the most part, otherness remained a demon of the imagination.

Notes

1. He is seen as a sort of premodern counterpart to the eighteenth-century European rationalist, able to see beyond particularity to the One.

2. Among some Ṣūfīs, say, or among Greek-influenced Muslim thinkers uncomfortable with the idea of a God so free as to be unconstrained by the laws of rationality.

3. His putative link to a royal bloodline, including both Lunar and Solar dynasties.

4. Near Pratapgad, on the road to Mahabaleshwar, one does find the Rāmavaradāyinī temple in which a mural depicts both Rāma and the beneficent goddess Rāmavaradāyinī, side-by-side with Śivājī and the goddess Bhavānī.

5. In other words, a 'Muslim,' since Muslims do not pierce the ears of young boys.

6. In Bengal, for very special ecological and historical reasons, a large percentage of the population converted to Islam.

7. 'Some Kṣatriyas are maintained [like Śāhajī], but more are killed by Muslims in battle.'

8. That is, 'path of those with unpierced ears,' a phrase with Sanskrit alliteration but suggesting the Islamic notion of path, Arabic *sharīʿah*.

9. That is, how one identified him- or herself as a Hindu or Muslim; how one employed a category like religion, Hinduism, or Islam; and, how one evaluated the religious identity of others.

10. Tulpule describes the unusual conversion of a Qādirīya Muslim known as Muntojī to Hinduism. He was renamed Mṛtyunjay, under which name he authored several Advaita works. It is noteworthy that his tomb is revered by people who still refer to him by a Muslim name (cf. Tulpule 1979: 363–64;

Ḍhere 1994: 1–37).

References Cited

Bhaktavijaya. 1995. *Stories of Indian Saints: Translation of Mahīpati's Marathi Bhaktavijaya* (trans. Justin Abbott and N. R. Godbole). Delhi: Motilal Banarsidass.

al-Bīrūnī, Abū Rayḥān. 1971. *Alberuni's India* (ed. Ainslee Embree). New York: Norton.

Citnis, M. R. 1924. *Śakakarte Śrī Śiva Chatrapati Mahārāja* (ed. K. N. Sane). Pūne: Āryabhūṣaṇa.

Ḍhere, R. C. 1994. *Ekātmatece Śilpakār.* Pūne: Mañjul Prakāśana.

Eaton, Richard M. 1993. *The Rise of Islam and the Bengal Frontier, 1204–1760.* Berkeley: University of California Press.

Ernst, Carl. 1992. *Eternal Garden: Mysticism, History, and Politics at a South Asian Sufi Center.* Albany: State University of New York Press.

Hacker, Paul. 1957. "Religiöse Toleranz und Intoleranz im Hinduismus." *Saeculum* 8: 167–79.

Hacker, Paul. 1983. "Inklusivismus." *In* Gerhard Oberhammer, ed., *Inklusivismus: Eine indische Denkform,* 11–28. Vienna: De Nobili Research Library.

Halbfass, W. 1983. "'Inklusivismus' und 'Toleranz' im Kontext der indo-europaischen Begegnung." *In* Gerhard Oberhammer, ed., *Inklusivismus: Eine indische Denkform,* 29–60. Vienna: De Nobili Research Library.

Kane, P. V. 1968–77 [1930–62]. *History of Dharmaśāstra.* 5 vols. Poona: Bhandarkar Oriental Research Institute.

Karve, Iravati. 1988. "'On the Road': A Maharashtrian Pilgrimage." *In* Eleanor Zelliot and Maxine Berntsen, eds., *The Experience of Hinduism,* 142–71. Albany: State University of New York Press.

Keḷkar, Y. N. 1928. *Aitihāsika povāḍe.* Vol. 1. Pūne: Tilak Mahārāṣṭra Vidyāpīṭa.

Keḷkar, Y. N. 1961. *Aitihasika povāḍe.* Vol. 3. Pūne: Tilak Mahārāṣṭra Vidyāpīṭa.

Laine, James W. 1995. "Śivājī as Epic Hero." *In* Günther D. Sontheimer, ed., *Folk Culture, Folk Religion and Oral Traditions as Components in Maharashtrian Culture,* 1–24. New Delhi: Manohar.

Laine, James W. 1996. "Śivājī's Mother." *In* Anne Feldhaus, ed., *Images of Women in Maharashtrian Literature and Religion,* 97–113. Albany: State University of New York Press.

Manusmṛti. 1991. *The Laws of Manu* (trans. Wendy Doniger, with Brian K.

Smith). New Delhi: Penguin Books.

Nandy, Ashis. 1998. Fraternal Violence. Lecture at the University of Minnesota, October 25.

Nānivḍekar, Śāhīr M. N. 1959. *Chatrapati Śivājī Mahārāj yāmcā povāḍa.* Bombay: Nānivḍekar Śāhīrī Saṅgam.

Oberhammer, Gerhard. 1983. "Der Inklusivismus-Begriff P. Hackers: Versuch eines Nachwortes." *In* Gerhard Oberhammer, ed., *Inklusivismus: Eine indische Denkform*, 93–113. Vienna: De Nobili Research Library.

Patwardhan, R. P., and H. G. Rawlinson, eds. 1929. *Source Book of Maratha History.* Bombay: Government Central Press.

Pollock, Sheldon. 1993. "Rāmāyaṇa and Political Imagination in India." *Journal of Asian Studies* 52, 2: 261–97.

Santavijaya. 1928. *Santavijaya of Mahīpati.* Muṁbaī: Induprakāśa Chāpkhānā.

Sardesai, G. S., ed. 1927. *Śivājī Souvenir.* Bombay: Tercentenary Celebration

Sarkar, Jadunath, ed. 1978. *House of Shivaji: Studies and Documents on Maratha History.* New Delhi: Orient Longman.

Sarvadarśanasaṃgraha. 1978. *Sarvadarśanasaṃgraha of Mādhava.* Pūne: Bhandarkar Oriental Research Institute.

Śivabhārata. 1927. *Śivabhārata of Paramānanda* (eds. D. V. Apte and S. M. Divekar). Pūne: Bhārata Itihāsa Saṃśodhaka Maṇḍala.

Smith, Jonathan. 1992. Differential Equations: On Constructing the 'Other.' Thirteenth Annual University Lecture in Religion, Arizona State University.

Tulpule, Shankar Gopal. 1979. *Classical Marathi Literature.* Wiesbaden: Otto Harrassowitz.

Conclusion

Catherine B. Asher

The four chapters by Stewart Gordon, Phillip B. Wagoner, Tony K. Stewart, and James W. Laine in this volume, along with Peter Gottschalk's introduction, are a welcome addition to studies challenging the widely held notion that the categories of Hindu and Muslim and/or Hinduism and Islam are binary. For many, these two categories have been the major driving forces for everything in the Indian subcontinent from the late twelfth century, including the creation of literature, art, and architecture to the implementation of political systems. As Gottschalk states in his introduction, the category of religion is seen by Western scholars— and, we might sadly add, by many contemporary South Asians—as fixed and divisive. The tendency is to envision South Asian society as divided along religious lines into two rigid and opposing camps. Incidents such as the 1992 destruction of the so-called Babri Masjid in Ayodhya by right-wing Hindu groups, the Vishwa Hindu Parishad's ongoing attempts to build a Rāma temple on the site of the former mosque, and the very recent communal riots of March 2002 in Gujarat are clear examples of this tension. These events were driven by groups in opposition to one another, each of which defines itself in terms of religion; but as the chapters in the volume explore, this is a modern construct, not one of the medieval and early modern period. Gottschalk's introduction suggests reasons for this understanding in current scholarly terms that include the traditional training in Western graduate programs that produce students who study things Hindu or things Muslim, but rarely both, in part due to language skills as well as the job market. That all of this, including contemporary attitudes in South Asia today, comes out of a colonial legacy as discussed by Gottschalk is well known from the work of scholars, including Partha Chatterjee (1993), Bernard Cohn (1996), Thomas Metcalf (1994), and Peter van der Veer (1994), among many others.

By contrast to an understanding of Indian history on communalist terms, the authors of these chapters argue that in medieval and early modern India identities were marked by relationships that shifted fluidly rather than the binary model of opposition assumed in so much scholarship. Building on the pioneering work of scholars such as Cynthia Talbot (1995) and Brajadulal Chattopadhyaya (1998), who have argued that the identity of peoples in medieval and early modern India was perceived rarely along religious lines but rather in ethnic terms, these chapters seek to understand identity perception through romances (Stewart), historical documents (Gordon, Laine, Wagoner), ballads and historical epics (Gordon, Laine, Wagoner), inscriptions and even architecture (Wagoner). Chapters written by Laine and Gordon concern the seventeenth- and eighteenth-century Marāṭhās. Stewart's contribution probes interpretations of Satya Pīr literature in Bengal, while Wagoner looks at social custom and behavior in the Deccani courts from the fourteenth through the sixteenth centuries. Thus we can think of these chapters as touching on the eastern and western parameters of the subcontinent as well as a southern one where considerable interaction occurred among people who happened to be Hindus or Muslims. Would we see similar situations to those outlined here in North India as well were this area included in the volume? The answer is surely yes, as I will indicate in my discussion that follows.

Gordon and Laine are both concerned with continuities and changes in political and patronage systems that occurred as territory shifted from ʻĀdil Shāhi and Mughal control to that of an independent Marāṭhā state. By examining detailed revenue documents, Gordon argues that overall patronage systems essentially remained unchanged and the Marāṭhā government continued to endow existing Muslim institutions and the worthy Muslim men who had been patronized under the earlier regimes, while at the same time enhancing the endowment of temples and other institutions associated with Hinduism. Private patronage, similar to that seen under the earlier Mughal and ʻĀdil Shāhi houses, continued as well, but in this case changes occurred in the building types that benefited due to the inclinations of new officials who replaced older ones. That is, as Marāṭhā and Brāhmaṇas supplanted the former ʻĀdil Shāhi military elite, who had been responsible for endowing the area with Muslim institutions, the patronage of this new elite was no longer extended to *madrasās*, *dargāhs*, and the like but now to temples and associated charities. However, as Gordon indicates, this shift was not religiously motivated, for precisely the same pattern was followed when Marāṭhā officials replaced Rājpūt ones. As he says, 'Conquest and state control were the goals; religion was no issue' (p.23).

Gordon goes on to argue that it is virtually impossible to equate the Marāṭhā state with a Hindu state. In fact, he points out that the Marāṭhā state had no single concept of legitimacy but three competing ones, underscoring the fluid nature of the seventeenth- and eighteenth-century Marāṭhā polity. There existed a sense of universal kingship under which the obligation of the ruler was to promote peace and prosperity. Similar documents exist in the larger Islamic world, for example, the many *adab* texts on kingship that had been produced from at least the eleventh century into the period under discussion. The general message of these texts was understood by large segments of society. A second sense of legitimacy derived from that fact that Marāṭhā elite had traditionally served as warrior families under the Mughals in the Deccan; in this sense, they are part of a larger Islamicate system described in the chapters by Laine and Wagoner. Another derived from Marāṭhā vision in which these kings saw themselves as the upholders of *dharma*. This included their responsibility to protect deities, Brāhmaṇas, and cows. In literature, for example the *Śivabhārata*, Muslims are demonized only rhetorically. This text, commissioned by Śivājī in conjunction with his coronation, deals with the ruler as dharmic king. As Laine points out, the text demonizes Muslims only because they do not protect gods and cows and, thus, fail to uphold *dharma*.

I would argue that the demonizing of Muslims in texts written for Hindu rulers is parallel to chronicles written for Muslim warriors, often rulers, who claim to have killed many Hindus and destroyed numerous temples. Both are legitimizing documents. In the Hindu document the ruler is an ideal one, yet, in reality, the other two forms of kingship cited by Gordon are more important than serving as a dharmic ruler. Laine indicates the difficulty the author of the *Śivabhārata* had, while on one hand presenting him as the upholder of *dharma* and demonizing Muslim actions against cows, god, and Brāhmaṇas, but at the same time tracing the rise of Śivājī's predecessors in the Muslim courts of the Deccan. Here, Laine notes, interaction with Muslims is normative and natural. By the same token, Muslims warriors who, according to texts, kill Hindus and destroy temples in reality could little afford to alienate a people so thoroughly, since Hindus as well as Muslims were needed to populate the warriors' armies. This is not to claim such destruction did not exist, but to assume wide-scale destruction as is usually the case is flawed as recent work by Richard Eaton (2000) has shown. In the seventeenth and eighteenth centuries the rhetorical devices of demonizing Muslims and Hindus existed more on paper than in the reality of daily life; by the nineteenth century and into the twenty-first century, this demonization has taken on a more serous nature.

The three chapters that are concerned with specific political entities make clear that none of these states, especially Vijayanagara and the Marāṭhā state, operated, as is believed in the popular imagination, as Hindu states ruled by Hindu rulers for the benefit of Hindu subjects. The same holds true for other contemporary states in North India, for example, the Kachavāhā domain of Jaipur. Many hold that when the city of Jaipur was founded in 1727 by Savāī Jay Singh it was conceived as a Hindu state rather than a state that happened to be ruled by a Hindu ruler. Here, personal piety (for Jay Singh was extremely religious and well versed in the *śāstras*) is confused with state polity. Jay Singh's sense of legitimacy was, like that of the Marāṭhās, three pronged. He still served his Mughal overlords; he had a keen sense of being a dharmic king, but his poets, unlike those of Śivājī, did not demonize Muslims. Rather, texts praising Jay Singh establish him as a universal ruler under whom peace and prosperity prevail (see Roy 1978).

Jay Singh saw himself as a champion of Brāhmaṇical causes and rights, but his state did not promote policies that discriminated against non-Hindus. He regarded himself as superior to the Mughals, who increasingly had become intolerant of public non-Muslim religious activity. Under the Kachavāhās, Jainas, for example, were major administrators and Muslims served the state as well. Jay Singh awarded Muslim *amīrs* with gifts and gave money to *dargāhs*, including that of Muʿīn al-Dīn Chishtī of Ajmer. When Jay Singh urged the Mughal ruler, Muḥammad Shāh, to desist taking the property of deceased mendicants, he included both Hindus and Muslims. Jay Singh did, however, have a policy of separate but equal. For example, he did not want Muslims involved in Hindu rites nor Hindu and Muslim holy men eating together as he considered this anti-Vedic. A contemporary poet, Girdhārī in his poem Bhojana-sāra, makes clear that Jaipur was a multicultural city. Toleration was practiced as he wrote: 'Nobody speaks improperly with any person.' He then goes on to say that 'in this city all the 32 weights are ... precise,' meaning justice prevails (cited in Roy 1978: 235–37). What the poet presents is a city ruled by a Hindu ruler where Brāhmaṇas are respected and temples are built, but at the same time Jaipur was a city intended as a universal city with multiple communities that could coexist peacefully. He then concludes: 'Everybody looks to his own religion (*dharma*), and all evil deeds are set aside' (cited in Gode 1946: 290). Thus in Jaipur as well as in the Deccan and in the Marāṭhā state, as the chapters in this volume show, Muslims might be regarded as different, to use Laine's terminology, but they are not other, for, as Gordon points out, 'neither Hindus nor Muslims defined themselves by what the other was not' (p.25).

In earlier work, Wagoner (1996) has shown how Islamicate dress and titles were adopted by the rulers of Vijayanagara to indicate that they were equal to the Shāhs and Sulṭāns of the larger Islamic world. In this volume, Wagoner studies two Muslim elite active in the various courts of the Deccan. This chapter reveals misunderstandings that arise when the contemporary language of communalism is imposed on medieval and early modern India. A case in point is the mosque built in 1439 by Aḥmad Khān in the Vijayanagara capital. Only the presence of a *miḥrāb* and its orientation toward Mecca give clues that it is a mosque, for it is not termed a mosque. Using the language of Vijayanagara courtly culture, it is termed a *dharmasāle* in its dedicatory inscription written in the local vernacular, Kannada. Moreover, the inscription employs the cultural language of traditional Indic inscriptions where the building is founded for the welfare of worshipers and for the ruler's merit. Not only is Indic terminology found in its inscription but also the mosque's appearance adheres to common Indic visual vocabulary. Like the Hindu and Jaina temples of Vijayanagara, the mosque is trabeated, that is, built on the post and lintel system. It adheres to the appropriate language for religious structures in the city. Yet, in spite of its Indic inscription and appearance, the users of Aḥmad Khān's *dharmasāle* understood perfectly its ritual purpose in the Muslim context. Those users and its patron, Aḥmad Khān, were able to perform cultural code switching and engage in boundary crossing, to use Wagoner's words, in an instant. Wagoner observes: 'If we arbitrarily decide to call it either a mosque or a *dharmasāle* alone, then we have fallen unwittingly into the intellectual straightjacket of communalism and failed to achieve our goal of a historical understanding of the past' (p.49). In order to understand medieval and early modern India on its own terms, Wagoner reminds us, we need to be able to engage in code switching and boundary crossing as naturally as did Aḥmad Khān when he constructed his mosque at the Vijayanagara capital. Gottschalk's introduction echoes Wagoner's observations.

The second noble whom Wagoner discusses, 'Ain al-Mulk Gīlāni, was also adept at code switching and boundary crossing. Knowledge of the military and cultural activities of 'Ain al-Mulk derive from several disparate sources including a Persian-language history, a Telugu chronicle, and inscriptions in Sanskrit. Together they tell of an elite military officer who was able to serve several Sulṭāns and Rājās. In each case 'Ain al-Mulk reached a high status on account of his military skill and ability to work in and move about accepted cultural spheres, Indic and/or Islamicate as well as shades in between, of any particular court. Not only was 'Ain al-Mulk able to communicate in the many languages used in the Deccani courts, but he also knew how to use these skills to his advantage. Perhaps there is no better case in point is 'Ain al-Mulk's request to the Vijayanagara *rājā* to donate a village that was part of 'Ain al-Mulk's landholding for the maintenance of Brāhmaṇas. As Wagoner notes, were he still serving the Bijapur Sulṭān the appropriate institution to endow would have been a *dargāh*; however, serving under the auspices of a Hindu king, 'Ain al-Mulk grasped the appropriateness of endowing a village for Brāhmaṇas that would correspond to the *rājā*'s sense of dharmic kingship.

In Mughal India, parallels to the cases of both Aḥmad Khān and 'Ain al-Mulk Gīlāni might be seen in those of Rājā Mān Singh and the Khān-i Khānān 'Abd al-Raḥīm, who, like 'Ain al-Mulk, could both converse in multiple languages and wear multiple cultural hats. For Mān Singh it depended on whether he was acting in the capacity of a Mughal *manṣabdār* or as the *rājā* of his own Kachavāhā house. Mān Singh and the Khān-i Khānān also understood the benefit of patronage that would find approval with their Mughal overlord, Akbar, and his political agendas. For example, Mān Singh constructed a mosque at the newly founded Mughal capital of Rājmahal as a way to show Mughal authority. This message was aimed at Afghans who had rebelled against the Mughals. Mān Singh also built a garden, Vāh, that could be read on two levels depending on which code was understood by which user. The garden's appearance, centering around a clear sparkling natural spring and bedecked with lovely pavilions, adhered to that of a typical Mughal pleasure garden. The tank and setting at Vāh was appreciated by the Mughal emperor, Jahāngīr, and his successors, as well as their nobility, as an appropriate Mughal pleasure retreat. But to Mān Singh personally, who knew that the gods, in this case Hindu, were attracted to the waters, waterfalls, trees, and spring-fed tanks, this garden, built in thanksgiving for Mān Singh's military victory and advancement within the Mughal system, must have evoked a more personal meaning. This meaning is one that would be readily recognized by other Rājpūt princes with whom he often served and, more often, served under Mān Singh (see Asher 1992, 1996).

The Khān-i Khānān's patronage of a sumptuously illustrated *Rāmāyaṇa* also reflected his ability to understand the multiple hats a productive noble was required to wear in order to further the agenda of the Mughal emperor, Akbar. This Mughal ruler wanted Hindu texts to be translated into Persian to encourage good relations among all subjects. The translations were imperially sponsored, but leading men such as the Khān-i Khānān provided illustrated copies that would better help spread knowledge of these texts than simply the written word (see Seyller 1999). While the audience would be limited to the elite few, it was, in fact, this body of men whom Akbar wished to influence, for they were the key to administrative reform.

While 'Ain al-Mulk, as Wagoner relates, is never identified directly as a Muslim in texts, and his religious tag is known only through his name, Mān Singh is identified as a Hindu in some contemporary texts; however, it is clear that 'Ain al-Mulk Gīlāni, Aḥmad Khān, Khān-i Khānān 'Abd al-Raḥīm, and Rājā Mān Singh functioned brilliantly not because of any religious convictions they might have held but because of their abilities to operate as military elite who moved seamlessly between Indic and Islamicate worlds. For them, engaging in 'cultural code switching' and 'boundary crossing' was second nature.

Stewart's chapter on the Satya Pīr romance tradition is also a study in code switching and boundary crossing. Unlike the chapters discussed earlier, this one is not about historical people or events; rather, it is about a rich Bengali literary tradition that is rarely studied. The reason for this, Stewart contends, is that it is not possible to classify the characters and their worlds into the tight categories of Hindu and Muslim. When romances such as *Lālmon* are discussed, they are usually considered to be products of syncretism. Stewart convincingly argues that to simply apply this label loses the complexity and complicated world of these Bengali narratives. Literature even more than life allows the categories of Hindu and Muslim to become subverted. These are stories that are addressed to no single audience, but Hindus and Muslims alike. While the main characters in *Lālmon*, the focus of Stewart's study, are princes and princesses, the intended audience includes ordinary people who are entertained by supernatural events and happy endings.

Stewart suggests that the world of Satya Pīr romances are not about religion, although religious traditions, both Hindu and Muslim, are suggested in the stories. For example, references are made to the popular snake goddess Manasā by the mention of a heroine associated with that story, but the reference is not to any religious aspect but to the heroine's ability to restore life to the dead. So, too, the hero's name, Ḥusayn, clearly alludes to both the Shīʿa and larger Islamic tradition, but never is the story about religion per se.

Romances such as *Lālmon* open up a world of possibilities. According to Stewart, the author, Kavi Āriph, is presenting us with a series of questions which commence with the phrase, 'what if?' What if, for example, women had more power in the world than men? He argues that the world Kavi Āriph portrays is similar to the real world, one that 'demonstrates the complexity of different forms of power with which people must be content' (p.82).

Thus the chapters in this volume urge us to reconsider the simple and rigid application of categories such as Hindu and Muslim when studying South Asia's medieval and early modern past. They argue for a complication of the binary we usually apply in historical, art historical, and literary studies of this period. We need to think of people living not in a single domain but sliding in and out of worlds, often like the characters in *Lālmon*, who have feet in more than one realm at a single time. As Gottschalk reminds us, we need to interrogate and disrupt modern understandings of Hindu and Muslim as categories; we consciously need to realize that those constructions as we understand them today do not apply to the subcontinent's earlier literature and history. It is only by doing this that we can understand the past and, perhaps, help prevent the dangerous rewriting of Indian history. Without making a serious attempt to understand a textured nuanced past, how can we hope to change the direction of communalism in India's future?

References Cited

Asher, Catherine B. 1992. "The Architecture of Raja Man Singh: A Study of

Sub-imperial Patronage." *In* Barbara Stoler Miller, ed., *The Powers of Art: Patronage in Indian Culture*, 183–201. Delhi: Oxford University Press.

Asher, Catherine B. 1996. "Gardens of the Nobility: Raja Man Singh and the Bagh-i Wah." *In* Mahmood Hussain, Abdul Rehman, and James L. Wescoat, eds., *The Mughal Garden: Interpretation, Conservation, Implications*, 61–72. Lahore: Ferozsons.

Chatterjee, Partha. 1993. *The Nation and Its Fragments: Colonial and Post-colonial Histories*. Princeton: Princeton University Press.

Chattopadhyaya, Brajadulal. 1998. *Representing the Other?: Sanskrit Sources and the Muslims (Eighth to Fourteenth Century)*. New Delhi: Manohar.

Cohn, Bernard S. 1996. *Colonialism and Its Forms of Knowledge: The British in India*. Princeton: Princeton University Press.

Eaton, Richard M. 2000. *Essays on Islam and Indian History*. New Delhi: Oxford University Press.

Gode, P. K. 1946. "Two Contemporary Tributes to Minister Vidhyadhara, the Bengali Architect of Jaipur at the Court of Sevai Jaisingh of Amber (A.D. 1699–1743)." *In, Dr. C. Kunan Raja Presentation Volume: A Volume of Indological Studies*, 285–94. Madras: The Adyar Library.

Metcalf, Thomas R. 1994. *Ideologies of the Raj*. Cambridge: Cambridge University Press.

Roy, Ashim Kumar. 1978. *History of the Jaipur City*. New Delhi: Manohar.

Seyller, John W. 1999. *Workshop and Patron in Mughal India: The Freer Ramayana and Other Illustrated Manuscripts of 'Abd al-Rahim*. Washington, D.C.: Artibus Asiae.

Talbot, Cynthia. 1995. "Inscribing the Other, Inscribing the Self: Hindu-Muslim Identities in Pre-colonial India." *Comparative Studies in Society and History* 37, 4: 692–722.

van der Veer, Peter. 1994. *Religious Nationalism: Hindus and Muslims in India*. Berkeley: University of California Press.

Wagoner, Phillip. 1996. "Sultan among Hindu Kings: Dress, Titles, and the Islamicization of Hindu Culture at Vijayanagara." *Journal of Asian Studies* 55, 4: 851–80.

Index

About the Editor and Contributors

Catherine B. Asher is an Associate Professor in the Department of Art History at the University of Minnesota, where she teaches Indian and Islamic art. She is the author of *Architecture of Mughal India* (Cambridge, 1992) and coeditor, with Thomas R. Metcalf, of *Perceptions of South Asia's Visual Past* (AIIS/Oxford, 1994). In addition, she has written many articles on Indian art and architecture.

Stewart Gordon works on political, military, and social history of precolonial South Asia. His specialty is Marāṭhā history, and he is the author of *The Marathas* (Cambridge, 1993) and *Marathas, Marauders, and State Formation in Eighteenth-Century India* (Oxford, 1994). His most recent work is a trans-regional study of ceremonial investiture in the Medieval period.

Peter Gottschalk examines the intersections of identity formation and the construction of knowledge among Hindus and Muslims in North India. He is the author of *Beyond Hindu and Muslim* (Oxford, 2000) and co-designer of "A Virtual Village" (www.colleges.org/~village). He is currently Visiting Assistant Professor in the Department of Religion at Wesleyan University in Connecticut while on leave from Southwestern University in Texas, where he is Assistant Professor.

James W. Laine is the H. Arnold Lowe Professor of Religious Studies at Macalester College in Minnesota. He is the author of *The Epic of Shivaji* (Orient Longman, 2001) and *Shivaji: Hindu King in Islamic India* (Oxford, 2003).

Sushil Mittal is Assistant Professor of Religion, the holder of the John C. Griswold Distinguished Professorship in Religion, and the Coordinator of

Gandhi Studies Program at Millikin University in Illinois. He is the editor of the *International Journal of Hindu Studies* (World Heritage, 1997). Current works under preparation include a biography on Mahātmā Gandhi, entitled *Mohandas Gandhi: A Biography* (Greenwood), and edited volumes, with Gene R. Thursby, entitled *The Hindu World* (Routledge), *Religions of South Asia* (Routledge), and *A Handbook for the Study of Hinduism* (Routledge).

Tony K. Stewart is Professor of South Asian Religions at North Carolina State University and the Director of the North Carolina Center for South Asia Studies, an educational cooperative of NCSU, Duke, UNC-CH, and NCCU. His specialty is medieval Bāṅglā literature and religion, having worked extensively in both Hindu and Islamic traditions. He has edited Edward C. Dimock's translation of the *Caitanya Caritāmṛta* of Kṛṣṇadāsa Kavirāja (Harvard, 1999). Current works include a volume of Satya Pīr folktale translations, entitled *Fabulous Females and Peerless Pīrs* (Oxford, in press), and a translation, with Chase Twichell, of Nobel Laureate Rabindranath Tagore's Vaiṣṇava poetry, entitled *The Lover of God* (Copper Canyon, in press).

Phillip B. Wagoner is Professor of Art History and Archaeology at Wesleyan University in Connecticut. He was trained in Telugu and Sanskrit literature and South Asian archaeology and works on the architectural and cultural history of the Medieval Deccan. His publications include *Tidings of the King: A Translation and Ethnohistorical Analysis of the Rāyavācakamu* (Hawaii, 1993) and, with George Michell, *Vijayanagara: Architectural Inventory of the Sacred Centre*, 3 volumes (Booklovers India, 2001). He has also written extensively on the history of Indic/Islamicate cultural interaction in South India.

CPSIA information can be obtained at www.ICGtesting.com
Printed in the USA
LVOW13*2120170414

382227LV00004B/38/P

9 780739 106730